1. Mary's House

Mary's House

Mary's House

Mary Pyle: Under the Spiritual Guidance of Padre Pio

Dorothy M. Gaudiose

ALBA · HOUSE NEW · YORK

SOCIETY OF ST. PAUL, 2187 VICTORY BLVD., STATEN ISLAND, NY 10314

Library of Congress Cataloging-in-Publication Data

Gaudiose, Dorothy M., 1920 -
    Mary's house : Mary Pyle : under the spiritual guidance of
Padre Pio / by Dorothy Gaudiose.
      p. cm.
    ISBN 0-8189-0646-4
    1. Pyle, Mary, 1888-1968. 2. Converts, Catholic — Italy —
Biography. 3. Pio, padre, 1887-1968. 4. Capuchins — Italy —
Biography.   I. Title.
BX4668.P85G38   1993
282'.092 — dc20   '92-21401
[B]   CIP

Designed, printed and bound in the United States of
America by the Fathers and Brothers of the
Society of St. Paul, 2187 Victory Boulevard,
Staten Island, New York 10314, as part of their
communications apostolate.

© *Copyright 1993 by the Society of St. Paul*

PRINTING INFORMATION:

Current Printing - first digit 1 2 3 4 5 6 7 8 9 10 11 12

Year of Current Printing - first year shown
  1993   1994   1995   1996   1997   1998   1999   2000

PREFACE

IT'S difficult to write about Mary Pyle without writing about Padre Pio, the Stigmatist — and vice versa. Those of you who read my first book, *Prophet of the People: A Biography of Padre Pio*, have already discovered that. Those of you who read this book, *Mary's House (Mary Pyle: Under the Spiritual Guidance of Padre Pio)*, also will soon understand what I mean. Both individuals made a lasting impression on people from all parts of the world, and I was fortunate enough to experience firsthand the amazing depth and power of their great love for humankind and their undying spiritual devotion.

Just as my first book was a tribute to Padre Pio, this one is a memorial to Mary Pyle, or as she was known, "Maria, l'Americana." It is a testimony to her lifetime dedication to the cause of Padre Pio, under whose spiritual guidance she remained for forty-five years until her death. Although she lived modestly in terms of earthly possessions, she was born an American heiress, a relative of the Rockefeller family. Before becoming a disciple of Padre Pio, she worked for ten years as an interpreter for the famous Italian educator Dr. Maria Montessori, and she spoke five languages fluently: English, French, German, Italian, and Spanish. Born a Protestant, she became a convert to Catholicism while in the services of Dr. Montessori. On October 4, 1923, she met Padre Pio, and thus began her life in San Giovanni Rotondo.

I met Mary Pyle in June 1950 while on a journey with my two sisters to the monastery of Padre Pio in San Giovanni Rotondo. I found her in a rose-colored house on a hill below the monastery. On subsequent visits, I became better acquainted and eventually served as her secretary, helping her answer a daily flood of mail and generally assisting with her heavy work load. Mary Pyle performed countless functions every day such as greeting visitors, acting as an interpreter, and offering hospitality to the poor. The numerous accounts in this book describe the great variety of services she performed and the many charitable activities she was engaged in throughout her life.

The accounts narrated in this book are arranged, as much as possible, chronologically. They cover not only Mary Pyle's activities (e.g., Life in Mary's House) during her years of service but pertinent related matters (e.g., Padre Pio's Family) that further illuminate the world in which she worked each day. Also, it is inevitable that these anecdotes about Mary Pyle provide new insights into the life of Padre Pio. After all, few persons knew Padre Pio better than Mary Pyle. The following examples give you an idea of the scope of the accounts (see the table of contents for a full listing):

— *A Christmas Dinner*
— *Lucia and the Crucifix*
— *Mary Pyle as a Hostess*
— *Conversations with Padre Pio*
— *From Mary Pyle's Notebook*
— *A Typical Day*
— *The Mission Workshop*
— *Wartime*
— *Acts of Charity*
— *Mary's Generosity*
— *Mary Pyle and Her Franciscan Family*
— *Pope John XXIII's Pontificate*
— *Mary's Health Declines*
— *Words from Padre Pio about Mary Pyle*
— *Memories of Mary Pyle*

Because Mary Pyle's life was so intertwined with events at the monastery in San Giovanni Rotondo, the accounts are wide ranging. Yet this is above all a book about the life and times of Mary Pyle. You may find that some of the accounts are astonishing, perhaps even impossible. But the incidences are those that I witnessed; that I heard directly from Mary Pyle; that I learned from close, reliable associates of Mary Pyle; or that I gleaned from published, documented sources. Not only was her work an accepted reality, but her contribution was so extensive that the Capuchin Fathers in Italy hope to initiate efforts toward canonization.

I made several visits to Italy after my first meeting with Padre Pio and Mary Pyle in 1950, returning in 1954, 1958, and 1961. Since I was on a leave of absence from teaching duties in Pennsylvania in 1961-62, I was able to remain nine months that year and continue working as Mary Pyle's secretary. In 1966 I returned again for the summer but was dismayed to find that her health was failing. When I said good-bye to Mary Pyle that year, I was concerned but didn't realize that it was to be a final farewell.

Mary Pyle died on April 26, 1968, but clearly, she lives on vividly in the hearts and minds of those whom her generous spirit touched and those whose lives were forever changed by the enduring presence of Maria, l'Americana.

Dorothy M. Gaudiose

Lock Haven, Pennsylvania

TABLE OF CONTENTS

The Convert	1
Maria l'Americana	2
A Christmas Near Mary Pyle and Padre Pio	12
A Christmas Dinner	14
The Visitors	16
Lucia and the Crucifix	18
Pietro Cugino	19
The Cappucci Family	22
Five Members of Mary Pyle's Household	22
Mary Pyle as a Hostess	26
Dr. Maria Montessori	27
Padre Pio's Spiritual Children	28
Padre Pio's Prayer Groups	29
The Capuchin Monastery and Emanuele Brunatto	30
Pietrelcina	35
The Early Years	36
The Decision to Remain Near Padre Pio	45
Becoming a Member of the Third Order Franciscans	51
Mary Pyle Settles in San Giovanni Rotondo	52
Conversations with Padre Pio	54
Padre Pio the Confessor	55
Brother Leone	57
The Congregation of the Holy Office	58
Padre Pio's Letters	59

From Mary Pyle's Notebook	64
Father Constantino Talks about Mary Pyle	73
Life in San Giovanni Rotondo	74
Padre Pio's Family	75
An Episode in the Life of Padre Pio "Told Me by Padre Pio's Mother"	76
Preserving Even the Smallest Things	82
Mary Pyle and Padre Pio's Parents	84
"Go to Mary's House"	86
Mary Pyle's Compassion and Generosity	88
Brother Gerard Natala	90
Life in Mary's House	91
A Typical Day	94
Enrico Zeni	95
The Mission Workshop	96
Padre Pio and Rome	98
Confinement and Release of Padre Pio	100
Wartime	101
The Forgione Home	103
Life in Pietrelcina	104
Father Ezechia	106
Return to San Giovanni Rotondo	106
Hospitality to Soldiers	108
Acts of Charity	113
"Meditation on the Immaculate Conception"	116
Z'Orazio	119
Efforts on Behalf of Padre Pio	121
The Young Pilgrim	122
Mary's Hospitality	123
A Letter to Carmelita	124
Maria Winowska	125
Mary's Generosity	127
Another Letter to Carmelita	128
To Be Near Padre Pio	130

Assisting Youth 131
Padre Pio Celebrates Mass Outdoors 132
A Letter from Mary Pyle 133
A Trip to Paris to Study French 136
News of Graces 137
Padre Pio's Last Blessing 144
Eight Stories from Mary's Notebook 146

    Giovanni Da Prato 146
    The Ticket 148
    Love of God 149
    A Cure 150
    Countess Luisa Vairo 151
    The Blind Man 152
    The Trinitarian Padre Pio 152
    The Woman Who Fell Under
        The Weight of the Cross 154

Monsignor Damini 155
Pio Abresch 157
Fair Share 158
Gian Battista 159
The Beneficial Effect of Padre Pio's Ministry 161
Mary Pyle and Her Franciscan Family 161
Padre Pio's "Spiritual Daughter" 163
Mary Pyle's Faith in the Honesty of People 164
Gaetanina 165
Padre Pio and Our Lady of Fatima 167
Another Letter to Carmelita 169
Pope John XXIII's Pontificate 171
The 50th Anniversary of
    Padre Pio's Ordination 172
Father Karol Wojtyla 172
Illness 173

Mary's Health Declines	175
Spring 1968	178
Retrospective	180
Mary's Funeral	182
Words from Padre Pio about Mary Pyle	184
Memories of Mary Pyle	185

DEDICATION

This book is dedicated to His Holiness, Pope John Paul II, gloriously reigning, and in thanksgiving to God for giving to the world such a brilliant, courageous and loving pontiff.

Mary's House

The Convert — Maria l'Americana
(Mary the American)

SITUATED in the town of San Giovanni Rotondo, about 275 kilometers from Rome and some 15 kilometers from the Gulf of Manfredonia on Italy's eastern coast, is a small colony of "permanent strangers," people from various places, people who hold widely varying views. Almost all of them were converts of Padre Pio, the Stigmatist. Many who passed by shores of unbelief to those of faith had been influenced by this exceptional personality. One of these converts was an American, Mary Pyle.

Mary Pyle first went to Italy in 1913, to work for Dr. Maria Montessori. She was in the professor's service as an interpreter for ten years. Mary became a convert to Catholicism and in 1923 went with Rina d'Ergin, a friend, to San Giovanni Rotondo, where she met Padre Pio. The visit induced her to remain and embrace the Franciscan way of life.

Tall and sturdily built, with a ruddy complexion, Mary invariably dressed in a long, brown robe similar to those worn by monks. She often greeted guests in her dining room, where she was frequently to be found engaged in her favorite task: making altar bread for the monastery. She was called "Maria l'Americana" (Mary, the American), primarily because it helped avoid confusion among so many Marys, but also because that's what she was: an American, something of a rarity in that part of Italy at that time.

For forty-five years Mary Pyle lived near the monastery of Padre Pio, at the foot of a hill in a fourteenth-century villa nestled among silver-green olive trees. The main house of the villa, about a hundred meters from the monastery, with its arches and towers, resembles a small castle. The somewhat weatherbeaten house of rose-colored plaster looks out over almond trees, the Gulf of Manfredonia, and the great wheat fields of Foggia. This was the house of Mary Pyle. Like a seaport, it was open to all. The small house bore silent testimony to events of joy, sorrow, affection, mourning, events no longer private but that are known to many through its association with the luminous spirit of charity: Padre Pio of Pietrelcina. It was in San Giovanni Rotondo that Mary discovered her Catholic faith. Here for many years lived the father of Padre Pio, Orazio Forgione and frequent visits by his wife Maria Giuseppa (Mary Josephine) Di Nunzio Forgione. In this house, in a modest-sized room on the second floor, they both died, the mother in January 1929, the father in October 1946. It was their great desire to have their son near them at the time of their deaths, and their prayers were heard. In their agony they were watched over by their son and were comforted by his prayers.

Maria l'Americana

DURING the Holy Year of 1950, my sisters, Helena and Carmelita, and I were on a tour bus in Rome. Near us sat a young American seminarian. Carmelita mentioned to him that our next trip would be to the town of San Giovanni Rotondo, in the province of Foggia, where we would see Padre Pio, the Stigmatist. When the young man heard this, he told us of a visit he had made to the monastery and how he had been impressed by the devout manner in which Padre Pio celebrated the Holy Mass. As the seminarian got off the bus, he said: "When you are in San Giovanni Rotondo, be sure to get in touch with Mary Pyle. She is known as Maria l'Americana. Since you're Americans, too, you should find her a big help."

It was the first time I had heard her name. My initial reaction was one of puzzlement as to what an American woman was doing at the monastery. Because I could not think of an adequate answer, however, I dismissed the question from my mind, and we continued on our tour.

One day in August of that year, after a memorable meeting with Padre Pio, we found ourselves in the center of the town of San Giovanni Rotondo. Some young women were lounging nearby, and we asked them where we could find Mary Pyle. "Maria l'Americana?" they asked, and we said yes. Two of the girls, who appeared to be in their teens, then volunteered to take us to her. We followed them down a hill to a villa near the monastery.

A small stone wall with a wrought-iron gate screened a courtyard that led to the entrance of the house. "This is Mary's house!" one of the girls said. A moment later, we entered a large room furnished with a long wooden table, chairs along the wall, and a portable organ. Standing near the organ was a tall, heavyset woman with a round face and blue eyes. She wore a Franciscan monk's habit and sandals.

Our guides, who by now had learned our names, introduced us; and we were invited to stay for tea. After we had accepted and sat down, Mary Pyle asked us where we were from and about our trip to Italy. Then she told us about her life in her Franciscan house, where she had lived since 1923, about being a disciple of Padre Pio and adopting the Third Order Franciscan Capuchin habit that she wore, which consisted of a long brown tunic encompassed by a white cord from which hung a rosary and a chain with a wooden crucifix. Mary told us too, about some experiences of others with Padre Pio — for example, the Mass he celebrated at five in the morning.

Carmelita, Helena, and I marveled at Mary Pyle's account of

Padre Pio. We were hearing for the first time of his mystical powers, including the advice he gave penitents after their confession.

Fascinated with Mary Pyle, we were so caught up in our conversation with her that we would gladly have remained longer; but when some young girls arrived and Mary said she had to hold choir practice, we took our leave. It wasn't until later that we realized the impact Mary had upon us. Nor could we know then what association we — especially my older sister, Helena — would have with her.

When we saw Mary Pyle again the next morning, we told her how much we had been impressed with the Mass celebrated by Padre Pio. It seemed to us that in celebrating the Mass, Padre Pio re-lived the passion of Christ. Mary Pyle appeared pleased, both with our praise and with our enthusiasm. Soon, though, it was time for us to leave; and thus ended our first encounter with Mary Pyle. When we returned to the United States, Helena and I sent her packages of clothing and food.

Mary's answer came after a silence of several weeks. In her letter, Mary thanked us for the gifts and apologized for the long delay in replying; she had many visitors in the meantime, and there was a veritable mountain of mail yet to be answered. "However," she wrote, "I have often thought of you. From here, near our beloved Padre Pio, comes a prayer. . . . It is a privilege to know him. He miraculously heals people who have never seen or known him. For him, there is no distance; as souls, we can come close to him, especially through prayer, even if there is an ocean between us. . . . In a seperate envelope I am sending you some cards (showing) the Capuchin Monastery in Pietrelcina, Padre Pio's native town, in which I am interested. The church was consecrated in the month of June, and it is truly beautiful.

"When you come back, I will take you to see it. There are about thirty 'fratini' (little brothers) and future Capuchin fathers there, and how they do love candies."

When Helena and I next visited Padre Pio's monastery town, we became better acquainted with Mary Pyle and through her became deeply involved in the activities of the monastery. Mary's house, in fact, had become a branch of the monastery, and around her had formed a small community of Third Order Franciscans whose lives were regulated by the rhythm of the monastery: the Mass of Padre Pio near dawn, a light meal at noon, the friars' activities in the afternoon. It was (and is) a place where every friar in the province can find someone ready to help in whatever needs attention.

Mary Pyle possessed a soul that was truly filled with love for God. She would not have been able to bear all the manifestations of her charity were it not for the continual presence of God in her heart. She was a missionary in her charity and love for the souls of her fellow human beings. How many returned to the Church and its sacraments through her words and the example of her life! Her house could indeed be called the "House of Charity and Love of God."

To this title must be added that of "Franciscan." Rich like Saint Francis, first, she, like Saint Francis, detached herself totally from riches. Then she became a modern "Jacopa de'Settesoli," the wealthy Roman woman who aided Saint Francis. Mary Pyle became for Padre Pio and the brethren around him a twentieth-century Jacopa de'Settesoli.

The sorrows, persecutions, and triumphs of Padre Pio were her's as well. During our visit in the summer of 1954, we helped members of her household send printed forms to people around the world, assuring them of Padre Pio's prayers in their endeavors. Until then, the monks, to alleviate their own heavy load of correspondence, sent the forms to Mary Pyle for reply.

We also volunteered to help the women clean the seventeenth-century church where Padre Pio conducted services. Sometimes, when the monks sent for Mary to serve as interpreter for visiting Americans and she could not go, she would send my sister and me instead. It was there, at the church, that we experienced some of Padre Pio's unusual powers — for instance, the sweet, perfumed odor that we associated with him and his apparent ability to answer questions before they were asked.

These visits to the monastery town of San Giovanni Rotondo were to contribute to increasing our valuable friendship with this remarkable woman. As I recall my experiences, it was Mary Pyle who guided us to Padre Pio. During our occasional visits to San Giovanni Rotondo, Helena and I became better acquainted with the women of the monastery community, known as "le pie donne" (the holy women). The women were not so much holy women as holy terrors, fanatics whom Padre Pio managed to keep in line with his booming voice, whereupon they subsided and behaved for the time being. They were emotional, superstitious women who hurt and angered Padre Pio. They never missed one of Padre Pio's Masses, no matter the season of the year; at the same time, one could not help being amused at some of the ways they chose to demonstrate their beliefs. For instance, during the summer, when there was a heavy influx of pilgrims, the women would arrive for Mass five or ten minutes before the church doors were due to open. Then, instead of going to the end of the line, they would take up a position near the head of the "enemy column!" As the doors of the church opened, they rushed forward to secure the best seats, those in the front few rows. In the old church where Padre Pio often said Mass at the side altar, they would sometimes chain a chair or stool to the side altar rails the night before, the better to make their claim for a seat the next morning. One morning Padre Pio arrived to celebrate Mass, only to find two women bickering over a chair. "Behave yourselves!" he said to them. "There are two American bishops present at this Mass." Immediately the argument stopped and, for the duration of that Mass at least, "le pie donne" were well-behaved.

One summer, the wife of an ambassador from a country in South America informed all within hearing that during the "charge of the holy women," she had been bitten! We heard later that this distasteful incident was one of the reasons for Monsignor Maccari being sent by Pope John XXIII to investigate the activities at San Giovanni Rotondo concerning Padre Pio.

How did Mary Pyle cope with the women? She was protected by a member of her household. I noticed that one of them would come early and take a front seat. Then, when Mary arrived, the woman would give up her place to Mary. Thus, Mary Pyle was never subjected to the women's unseemly wrangling. Over the years, as some of the women became beneficiaries of Mary's charity, one or another "pia donna" even made room for their benefactress!

The most memorable encounter I had with Mary Pyle, however, came in 1961-62, when I took a sabbatical from teaching and spent my leave in Europe. Helena, now a widow, accompanied me on the trip. Upon arriving at Padre Pio's monastery town that September, we checked in at the Hotel Santa Maria delle Grazie (Saint Mary of the Graces) and began the process of acclimating ourselves to living abroad. After a few days we noticed that the activities surrounding Padre Pio included attendance at his early-morning Mass, which lasted an hour and a half; a visit at 11:00 to the church, to see Padre Pio at prayer in the choir loft; a benediction service at 4:00 p.m., conducted by Padre Pio, with Mary Pyle playing a pump organ; and finally, at 8:00 p.m., gathering in a field under a window of the monastery and waving our handkerchiefs, saying good night to Padre Pio, who would wave to us and give his blessing.

When we had observed these activites for a short while, Helena and I assessed the situation — or rather, of ourselves and our part in the life of the community that revolved around the monastery. We decided to try to do more, to become a more integral part of the community. Therefore, one morning after Padre Pio's early Mass, we went to discuss the matter with Mary Pyle. Telling her that we had noticed several baskets of mail in her workroom, we said we would like to work for her as volunteer secretaries, answering the English-language mail that she received.

Mary was delighted. "It's strange that you should say this to me at this time." she said. "Only this morning I said to Padre Pio: 'Padre, I am so bogged down with correspondence. I very much need someone to help me with it.' So, you see, I feel that both of you were sent to me by Padre Pio."

The day we started to work, we were shown into a small room on the second floor of her home. In the room were a cot, a writing desk, and three small tables with benches. On the wall were several photographs of Padre Pio and a font of holy water. Mary had "filed" the letters in bushel baskets labeled according to the language in which the letters were written. The number of letters in English far exceeded those in other languages. There were letters from English-speaking people in the United States, England, Ireland, Australia, India, and several countries of southern Africa. Most of the letters contained a request for prayers and an offering.

One morning Mary received a letter from L'Abbe Constantin, who lived in Paris. After she had read the letter, Mary said to us: "I must tell you about L'Abbe. He was the pastor of one of the churches of the city of Paris. His only close relative was his widowed mother, who was his housekeeper for many years. When his mother died from the infirmities of old age at about eighty, her son became emotionally upset. He decided, therefore, to come to San Giovanni Rotondo to see Padre Pio.

"At his first opportunity to speak with Padre Pio privately, L'Abbe told Padre Pio about his sorrow over the death of his mother. Padre Pio listened and said: 'Your mother died in the arms of Jesus. Live in such a manner that you too will be reunited with her in heaven.' " As L'Abbe later related the conversation to Mary, he was consoled by Padre Pio's words.

Helena experienced Mary's psychic ability as well. She had been told by her American doctor that she was in need of hernia surgery. Shortly after our arrival in Italy, Mary told her: "I was dreaming of you last night. I saw you being wheeled into the operating room. But before that was done, I saw Padre Pio tenderly covering you with a sheet." After thinking about Mary's words, one day my sister said to Padre Pio: "I know I need an operation; but I'm undecided whether to have it done in Italy or when I return to America." Padre Pio advised having it done in Italy. Thus, the surgery was performed about a month after Mary had told Helena of her dream.

My sister and I were often impressed, even amazed, upon hearing of Mary Pyle's experiences. Sometimes she related anecdotes of her work for Maria Montessori. Once, she said, she and Doctor Montessori had arrived in Rome very late in the day. The only rooms they could get were in a run-down hotel. All night long she was kept awake by streetwalkers coming and going in the next room.

Another time, she received a letter from a German woman who sent a donation and a request for the prayers of Padre Pio. "Oh, I remember this woman especially," Mary said; "she had come to Italy from Germany, and she kept saying, 'I came here for a little thing, a very little thing!' It turned out that the woman had come to gain the custody of her seven-year-old illegitimate son, who had been raised in Italy until she decided to take him home with her to Germany."

"Mary," I said, "as a teacher, I've had experience with illegitimates, and I've noticed that many are intelligent and attractive, as though these were gifts from God to help them through life."

"What you say may be true," Mary replied: "but Padre Pio says, 'Illegitimate children are born of passion, and are restless all their lives.' "

"At least the women had the children!" I said.

She nodded. "Yes, that is true." Mary also told us that Padre Pio believed that as far as morals were concerned, Paris was the sewer of the world. It was our great fortune to work with Mary Pyle. She was sweet-tempered and energetic. Helena and I began our workday at 9:00. After lunch, which usually lasted an hour, we returned to our task and worked until about 3:00. On some days, we considered ourselves fortunate to answer three letters. There were numerous interruptions in Mary's schedule: visitors to be greeted and escorted through the monastery, decisions to be made concerning one aspect of Mary's work, the poor who came for alms, or, as happened frequently, a letter from someone known to Mary, which brought back memories, and she would stop what she was doing and tell us about the writer of the letter.

Thus the world of Mary Pyle opened up for me, revealing a virtuous, compassionate woman, an outstanding person who, under the spiritual direction of Padre Pio, had set out to live the Christian life to its fullest.

In the replies she dictated to those who had written her, Mary obeyed Padre Pio explicitly, saying to the recipient only what she knew the padre would approve of. She was paraphrasing his thoughts. Since Helena and I were, in effect, replying on behalf of Padre Pio second or third hand, Mary at first reread all the letters she had dictated before she signed them — notwithstanding the extra work involved. She did this to assure herself that my sister and I had not inadvertently interjected our own thoughts. Later, she trusted us and did not check the letters. Those who received letters signed by Mary Pyle can rest assured that, while they were receiving the words of Mary Pyle, they were at the same time receiving the thoughts of Padre Pio.

Roux Garcin, whenever she visited San Giovanni Rotondo from Paris, used to help Mary with the correspondence that was in French. Commenting on Mary one time, Roux told Helena and me that, above all else, Mary was steadfast in her prayers, whether in church or privately, as well as in her work for the community. For instance, one day Roux asked Mary, who was sick in bed, why she didn't pray while seated on the bed. Mary answered: ''Because I do not want to fall asleep during my prayers." Roux Garcin said that during the festive days of the Church's calendar, having satisfied her obligation to hear Mass, she had wanted to skip the afternoon benediction services, to continue working, primarily because she had so many letters to answer; but Mary insisted that Roux go with the rest of the household to the afternoon benediction services.

Mary Pyle seemed close to her God. She was pleasant in her spiritual conversation. She lived hidden, intent on her work of charity, in the silence of her humility. Her preferred demeanor was that of reservation. In vain would the observer find her after services in extended conversation before the church. Situated on the mystical Gargano Mountain, Mary Pyle's habitat, with its motto of "Prayer and Work," resembled a monastery of devout souls, an enchanted hermitage. This place, this life, represented the essence of life to her.

Those who lived in the house with Mary lived a life of intense piety, one between the church and the house where a small community of devout people had formed: the spiritual children of Padre Pio. Their life of labor lay in service to the monastery, preparing the altar bread for the monastery and making the sacred vestments for the friars. Mary Pyle, the humble disciple of Padre Pio, was the guardian and promoter of the spiritual life of the house's inhabitants.

Mary led a life of charity and beneficence toward those in need. She loaned large sums of money from her considerable fortune, money that often was not repaid. But Mary never resorted to legal means to have the loans repaid. After all, she recognized, the great majority of those who borrowed from her had, in fact, come to her as impoverished people without the means to repay a loan, no matter how small.

In the view of the Capuchin Fathers, whenever the story of Padre Pio is told, no one writes anything about Mary Pyle that would tarnish her image, either directly or indirectly. When Mary

Pyle was a young woman, the member of a family that moved in what was then called "high society," her mother insisted that she dress stylishly, that she present herself in a manner suitable to her high social position. Mary, however, often neglected such matters. She was annoyed with her long but stylish hair and frequently rebelled when she was rebuked about her appearance.

By the time she had settled in at San Giovanni Rotondo, Mary had removed practically every vestige of her former life from her present, daily life. She had detached herself from every sign of vanity and ostentation. When she came to Padre Pio, for instance, she still owned jewelry, from which she felt — had, indeed, been told — she should divest herself. This she did, keeping only her wristwatch, because it served a functional purpose. The watch, though, was a very expensive one of gold and diamonds. Thus even this object became suspect. She was still undecided about keeping the watch when one day in the sacristy, as she and Padre Pio talked, he observed: "You still have the gold watch with the diamonds, eh?!" Immediately, Mary left the church and went to the monastery walk. There she took a stone, smashed the watch, and gathering up the fragments, returned to the sacristy, where she presented Padre Pio with the fragments.

A Christmas Near Mary Pyle and Padre Pio

THE Christmas that my sister and I spent near Padre Pio and Mary Pyle was a vivid one that we will remember as long as we live. On a starry, brisk Christmas Eve, shortly before 11:00, we left the hotel and walked the quarter mile to the monastery church of Saint Mary of the Graces. As we went up the road, we met others making their way to the church. A peasant couple dressed in native clothes attracted our attention; the woman had a black wool shawl wrapped around her, while the man (her husband?) wore a cape-like coat and a wide-brim hat. They reminded us of the biblical story of the First Christmas, of the shepherds hurrying to the stable at Bethlehem.

We reached the church, now filled nearly to capacity with worshippers, many of whom, I learned later, had come great distances, some from other parts of Europe and from around the world. All were there for Padre Pio's celebration of midnight Mass.

Helena and I walked quietly down the side aisle of the church to a portable organ. There, seated at the organ, was Mary Pyle, playing traditional Christmas carols that were being sung in Latin by the choir. As we stood near the organ, and between carols, Mary whispered to us that if we moved the music books and songsheets that lay on a bench near us, we would have a place to sit. So my sister and I placed our pocketbooks near Mary. We stacked the music books in a corner, and soon the bench was clear. When we went to take our seats on the bench, however, we were surprised to find five heavyset women occupying our seats. Seemingly no amount of persuasion would convince them to budge. As a result, we had to stand for Padre Pio's three Masses, which we knew he was scheduled to celebrate and which, we also knew, would last more than three hours.

Just before midnight, a procession led by Padre Pio began at the rear of the church. Slowly the procession approached the main altar. Padre Pio's face shone; it was radiant, luminous. He wore a cape and carried a pillow on which lay an infant doll. In his train were Capuchin monks, with their brown habits and white surplices, walking in pairs, carrying lighted candles and chanting in Latin.

It was almost precisely midnight when Padre Pio placed the effigy of the Infant Jesus above the tabernacle, in the place where the monstrance usually is placed during the benediction services. As he did so, and the choir sang "A Child Is Born," two choirgirls lit sparklers before the altar. As the choir sang, Padre Pio incensed the Infant — so heavily that he was almost obscured by the smoke. This part of the ceremony, of course, symbolizes the birth of Christ.

It was at this point that the Mass proper began. Padre Pio, as celebrant, was assisted by two priests; all three were dressed in gold-colored vestments. Padre Pio's celebration of the Mass, which took about an hour and a half, as usual was characterized by carefully placed pauses, clear diction, and tears as well as by the bleeding of his hands at the Consecration.

I noticed that few had left the church after midnight Mass. Most knew, as Helena and I did, that Padre Pio would likely go immediately into the second Mass. At that time, priests were permitted to celebrate three Masses at Christmas. So, when the first Mass was over, the assistant priests left Padre Pio and, alone and without singing, he began the second Mass at the altar.

At the end of this Mass, Padre Pio looked exhausted. A monk brought him a chair, on which he sat, and for a few minutes at the Gospel side of the altar, he rested his head. Padre Pio then celebrated his third Mass, this one in the same devout manner in which he had celebrated the preceding two. When he finished, he was so near exhaustion that he had to be assisted by two Capuchin priests.

It was now four-thirty in the morning, and Helena and I had been standing for five hours! As we walked down the road from the church, however, we agreed that we did not even feel tired.

A Christmas Dinner

MARY Pyle had invited Helena and me to have Christmas dinner with her and the members of her household. So, just before noon on Christmas Day, we arrived at Mary's house. With five other guests present, there was a flurry of activity, a flurry all the more noticeable because some were arguing about whose fault it was that some of the desserts that had been ordered had not been delivered.

At last everyone stood at the table for prayers. When everyone was settled and quiet, Mary took up a doll of the Infant Jesus and held it. She blessed everyone, especially those who had been bickering. After the blessing all became peaceful and calm, and the festive meal began. There was antipasto, pasta shells stuffed with meat, salad, and sweets, after which espresso coffee and wine were served. Thus, with singing and native dances by some of the women, the day passed quickly.

The next day, Padre Pio as usual celebrated his early-morning Mass; following the Mass, however, he collapsed from exhaustion and had to be taken to bed, where he remained for a week. The Father Superior of the monastery soon announced that Padre Pio would no longer celebrate three Masses at Christmas; it was too great a strain on him. The Christmas season of 1961, therefore, was to be the last time Padre Pio celebrated three Masses at one time.

One evening in February 1962, Helena and I were sitting in front of the fireplace at the Hotel Saint Mary of the Graces with Nancy, a friend from New York, sharing our experiences of Padre Pio. During the conversation Nancy informed us that she was leaving for England the next morning to visit her sister, who had moved there from Ireland. Our conversation was interrupted by the appearance of the desk clerk, who informed Nancy that she had a long-distance telephone call. Several minutes later, Nancy returned to her seat near the fireplace. Now her face was ashen. Clearly, she had been disturbed by the phone call. She said the call was from her son-in-law, who told her that a friend of the family, a thirty-three-year-old baroness, had committed suicide by jumping out the window of a building. We tried to console Nancy, to no avail. Finally, my sister said: "Tomorrow morning Padre Pio is to hear my confession. I will ask for words of consolation for you!" Helena's statement seemed to calm Nancy somewhat.

The next morning, Helena kept her appointment. I waited for her. When she came out of the confessional, she looked extremely disturbed. Her face bore a look of horror. As we walked together the short distance to the hotel, Helena told me what Padre Pio had said. She had, of course, mentioned the suicide of Nancy's friend and had told Padre Pio that Nancy was distraught. Could Padre Pio give Helena some words of consolation for her friend? Padre Pio replied heatedly: "The Baroness went directly to hell! You may tell your friend that I said so."

When we reached the hotel we found Nancy already packed, waiting for a taxi to take her to the train station. We said good-bye without Helena giving her Padre Pio's message. When I asked why Helena had not, she said she didn't have the heart to tell Nancy.

Later that morning we went to Mary Pyle's house to help her with her correspondence in English. During lunch, Helena told Mary Pyle about the death of Nancy's friend and what Padre Pio had said about it. When she was finished, Mary asked: "Helena, did you tell Nancy?" Upon hearing the answer, Mary was surprised but added: "Helena, if Padre Pio told you to do something, I recommend that you do it. Otherwise, why would you seek his advice?" Helena promised to write a letter to Nancy that same evening, telling her of Padre Pio's answer concerning the baroness's death.

Several months later, we met Nancy in New York. Nancy told us that Padre Pio's statement about the baroness's soul had changed her life. She no longer sought material wealth; in fact, since that time, she had made numerous contributions to charity! Helena reflected that she was grateful for Mary Pyle's advice.

The Visitors: Some Celebrities

BECAUSE Mary's house was open to everyone, my sister and I were presented to people from all walks of life: journalists, authors, concert pianists, composers, opera singers, doctors, lawyers, industrialists, bishops, emissaries from the Vatican, actors and actresses, and ordinary people.

One day Mary showed us three brown albums containing the collected autographs of visitors to Mary Pyle's house. Among them were celebrities not only from Europe but from other parts of the world as well. There were signatures, in various languages, with addresses and declarations of gratitude for the hospitality and help they had received from Mary Pyle or through her intervention. When we asked Mary how many signatures the albums contained, she replied. "Members of my household, who counted them, tell me there are over three thousand."

She asked us to sign the album, which we gladly did. Later, in looking for familiar names, we saw those of two American film stars, Loretta Young and Ramon Navarro.

Mary told us that when Miss Young was interviewed by reporters and was asked what had impressed her most during her European vacations, she replied: "The Mass celebrated by Padre Pio in San Giovanni Rotondo." Ramon Navarro said that after meeting Padre Pio, he no longer wanted to talk about his past life.

Padre Pio's Mass at 5:00 every morning was attended by nearly a thousand people, who came in all kinds of weather. When Padre Pio began to celebrate the Mass at the foot of the altar, excitement (even, for some, ecstasy) spread through the worshippers and held them spellbound. During the Mass, suffering shone through Padre Pio's features. All could see the painful contractions of his body, especially when he leaned on the altar and genuflected as though he bore the entire weight of the Cross. Tears rolled down his cheeks and from his mouth came words of prayer, of supplication for pardon, of love for his Lord, of whom he seemed virtually a perfect replica. The only time Padre Pio removed the fingerless gloves that covered the wounds in his hands was to celebrate the holy sacrifice of the Mass. At the consecration the wounds bled, and all those present noticed the passage of time. It took Padre Pio about an hour and a half to celebrate Mass, during which time attention was riveted on every gesture, movement, and facial expression of the celebrant.

Lucia and the Crucifix

ONE morning Mary Pyle gave Helena and me copies of a letter written by Lucia Fiorentino, a mystic who lived from 1889 to 1934. In 1906, at the age of seventeen, Lucia had a vision in which the arrival of Padre Pio in San Giovanni Rotondo was predicted. When he arrived in San Giovanni Rotondo ten years later, Lucia became one of his spiritual daughters, and her life was guided by him thereafter. Lucia's vision went like this:

> *I saw in a vision a tree of immeasurable size in the atrium of our Capuchin Friary, and heard a voice which said to me: "This is a symbol of a soul which is now far away but who will come to (you) and do much good in this town. . . . He will be strong and well rooted as this tree, and all souls which come to him — those of the town and elsewhere — if they take refuge in its shade will be freed from evil (that is, who comes to this priest to be enlightened, to find pardon and a remedy for their faults). If they humble themselves, they will receive counsel and fruit of eternal life from this worthy priest. Those who despise his counsel, his way of doing things, will be punished by the Lord in this life and in the next. His mission will go 'round the world. Many will take refuge in the shade of this mystical tree so as to have fruits of grace and forgiveness."* (Letters, vol. III, p. 420)

Mary then told us about Lucia Fiorentino and the Crucifix. At the time, there lived in San Giovanni Rotondo an old woman who was poor as well as blind and partly deaf. There was nothing in her life that could cheer her or from which she could obtain comfort except a small crucifix Padre Pio had sent her through Lucia Fiorentino, who felt sorry for this woman. The small crucifix was constantly in her hands, and she would cover it with kisses when she went to bed at night. The woman called it her "Padre Pio's Jesus Christ."

One evening the old woman began to weep and wail. "I have lost my Padre Pio's Jesus Christ! How can I go to sleep without my crucifix?" She called in her neighbors, who tried to comfort her. Her friends searched the house, looking everywhere, but could not find the crucifix. The woman's niece came to sleep with her as usual, but there was no sleep for the poor woman that evening; her heart was too heavy over the loss of her one and only treasure. At about two o'clock the next morning, the woman thought the front door had been opened. She felt a gust of wind, then the presence of someone near her. Suddenly she felt an object being placed in her hand. The door closed, and she was alone again. Her niece slept quietly at her side. Remembering the visitation, slowly she opened her hand and there saw the crucifix. Quietly she said to herself: "Padre Pio has brought me back my crucifix."

As soon as it was light, the old woman sent for Lucia and told her what had happened. Lucia's amazement knew no bounds, for the crucifix wasn't the original one but rather a new — or, at least, different — one, the type Father Pio had been giving away at the time. Lucia hastened up to the monastery and asked Padre Pio if he had given the old woman the crucifix. Father Pio merely replied: "She has her crucifix. Well, that suffices."

Pietro Cugino

IN appreciation for our services, Mary invited us to join her and her household for their noonday meal. At the table we noticed that

Mary extended hospitality to others, especially the poor who had come to visit Padre Pio and who had no place to stay. Consequently, in addition to her household staff of four women, there usually were twelve to fourteen others at the table.

Among them each day was Pietro Cugino, a blind, middle-aged man. Each member of Mary's household had an anecdote to tell which almost invariably concerned how they had been sent to Mary Pyle's house by Padre Pio. Pietro Cugino — or "Petruccio" (Little Peter) — as he was affectionately called — was an institution. He was a husky-looking young man about twenty-seven years of age, with a sunny disposition. Because the area was so familiar to him, he walked everywhere alone, using his cane. He never faltered or stumbled, and seemed to know every step, every obstacle, both indoors and out. Moving at a comfortable pace, he was greeted by everyone, and recognizing the voice of all who spoke to him, he called them by name as he returned their greetings.

Mary Pyle told us that Petruccio Cugino as a young boy had his sight and used to play around the monastery with the other boys of his age while his father visited with Padre Pio. One day, when this occurred, his father said to Padre Pio: "Tell Petruccio to think of more serious things — of what work he should do in life — instead of play." Padre Pio, who often seemed to foresee the future, said: "No, let him alone. Let him play now. The time will come when he will know what to do."

Mary continued. Petruccio gradually lost his sight and at the age of twelve became blind. One day he went to Padre Pio as a supplicant, seeking to have his sight restored. Padre Pio asked him: "Do you want to have your sight restored, or do you want to save your soul?"

It was a difficult choice for a strong young man to have to make. Petruccio said: "If it is strictly a choice, I should rather save my soul."

"It is strictly a choice," replied Padre Pio.

Padre Pio kept Petruccio beside him, and he became an accepted part of the monastery and of those connected with it. He went on errands, carried mail from the town to the monastery, and did everything he could to be helpful. Petruccio was given a place of honor every morning; he preceded Padre Pio from the sacristy when he came to say Mass and stood beside the altar, with his sightless eyes facing the altar and kneeling during the Consecration. Through the friendship and guidance of Padre Pio and his daily acceptance of the burden, which, he sensed, would never be lifted, Petruccio's face gradually seemed to glow as though from an inner light. His face took on the appearance of the face of a Christian martyr.

Each afternoon Petruccio went to visit Padre Pio in his room. It was through Petruccio that Mary asked for Padre Pio's advice about her affairs, her relatives and friends, and about those who had requested his advice through letters sent to her.

Petruccio told us a story about Mary Pyle. As a member of the Third Order Franciscans, Mary adopted the way of life of the Capuchins and observed their rules scrupulously. Even when she was at home, she observed every aspect of Lent, just as the Friars did. She was well versed in guarding the quality and the quantity of food taken according to the friar's dietary laws.

It happened that at that time, the forty days of Lent ended at noon on Holy Saturday. That year, the religious functions of the "resurrection" ended after the morning services. Mary returned from church about eleven that morning and, believing that Lent was over had coffee and sweetcakes. Later, in speaking with others, she learned that she had been mistaken about the end of Lent. Therefore, thinking she had done something grievously wrong, Mary wished to confess to Padre Pio. Sometime thereafter, she repeated Padre Pio's words to members of her household. "And at the end of Lent, you broke the rules," he had said in a shocked tone of voice. "How come? Didn't you know that the fast of Lent ends on Holy Saturday at noon, and not before?"

"How scrupulous Mary Pyle was in everything," Petruccio concluded; "while we the members of her household, were not as scrupulous!"

The Cappucci Family

IN 1927, a family by the name of Cappucci — mother, father, and their two daughters, Concetta and Adolorata — presented themselves to Mary Pyle, saying they wished to live there, to be near her and give her whatever assistance she needed. When Mary learned that Padre Pio had recommended that she take the family in, she did so at once. An entrance hall and stairway divided the house in two, with two rooms downstairs and two upstairs. The Capucci family lived on one side of the house.

By the time Helena and I arrived in 1950, the parents had died, and Mary Pyle had assumed the care of Concetta and Adolorata. Concetta was by then suffering from heart disease, and Adolorata had poor eyesight — which meant that neither sister could be of much service to Mary Pyle. Mary never complained about this situation, however, saying Concetta's and Adolorata's past years of help were enough.

Five Members of Mary Pyle's Household

AS mentioned, there were five women in Mary Pyle's household. They lived with her, making Mary's house their home while working for their room and board. Eventually I interviewed each of them concerning the life of Mary Pyle. They were: Carmela

Mary Pyle: Under the Spiritual Guidance of Padre Pio   23

Marrocchino, Catherina Valenti, Maria Tagliavia, and Franca Petrucci. As sometimes happens, these women quarreled among themselves. When that happened, Mary would plead with them, saying: "We live under the same roof. We eat at the same table and partake of the same bread. Why can't you love one another?" Mary carefully avoided becoming angry with them; she merely wanted them to settle their differences and to love one another.

Carmela Marrocchino, a woman of medium height and weight, had brown hair and dark brown eyes. Carmela had come to San Giovanni Rotondo in 1937. She met Mary Pyle and remained in Mary's household until 1942, when Mary left San Giovanni Rotondo and went to Padre Pio's family in Pietrelcina, whereupon she returned to her hometown of Canosa. In 1952, she returned to Mary Pyle and remained with her until Mary's death. Carmela continued to live in Mary's house, which had been willed to the Capuchin order.

When she arrived in 1937, Carmela said, she found living in Mary's house Catherina Valenti, a cook for Mary and her guests. Catherina was German by birth; she had married an Italian and they had come to Rome to live. When her husband abandoned her, she came to meet Padre Pio and, then, Mary Pyle. Mary gave her lodging in her house, and Catherina remained with her for more than thirty years until Catherina's death in 1966. According to Carmela, Catherina, though basically a good person, often tried the patience of Mary and others in the household by behaving as though she were the proprietress and by a tendency to be suspicious of people.

Maria Tagliavia, or "Maria of Sicily," as she was called — a short, stocky, dark-haired woman who had come from Salemi, Sicily in the early 1950s — remained with Mary for about sixteen years. She would often abstain from eating certain foods as a form of penance. One day Mary Pyle said to her: "Blessed are you, Maria, for all the acts of penance you perform!" "And blessed are you, too!" Maria replied. "When you die, you will be covered with the blanket of charity. I am not able to do charity, so when I die, I will be covered with the blanket of penance!"

When Maria Tagliavia, for reasons of health, was going to leave the household of Mary Pyle to return to Salemi, someone suggested to Mary Pyle that she sign a declaration stating that Maria Tagliavia had worked for her as a house servant for sixteen years; that would enable Maria to obtain a modest pension. Mary refused, however, saying: "I cannot because she had been in my house as a guest like the others, and not as a domestic."

Another member of Mary's household was Tonina Teglia. Tonina, a slight, not strong girl with dark hair, black eyes, and an olive complexion, limped slightly from one leg being shorter than the other. Soon after her arrival at Mary's house, Tonina said, she fell ill with pleurisy, which developed into tuberculosis; and she was confined to bed. Mary Pyle helped Tonina with everything. Not wishing anyone to avoid Tonina for fear of contagion, Mary herself purchased and administered all the necessary medication, and she saw to it that Tonina's clothes, bed linens, and towels were kept separate. Months later, largely through Mary Pyle's ministering, Tonina recovered from the disease.

Among the first things Tonina did was thank Padre Pio for his prayers, which had been made through Mary's request. When Tonina later met Padre Pio, he said: "Behold, I myself have saved you. You were supposed to die. But I have saved you!"

Franca Petrucci was the chief cook of Mary's household. She was a heavyset woman of medium height, with a hearing problem. Franca had worked as a cook in a hotel in Rome, where she had often served Mary Pyle and her mother. When Franca came to see Padre Pio, she learned that Mary Pyle had a house and was living near the monastery.

Franca said she made a habit of staying at Mary's house every time she came from Rome to San Giovanni Rotondo for spiritual direction from Padre Pio. Once when she was ill, she had come to Padre Pio asking for his prayers for relief from the illness. Padre

Pio helped her regain her health, and she returned to thank him, as well as to tell him she was no longer a cook in Rome.

The next day in church she met Mary Pyle, who embraced her, saying: "Franca, you must come to my house!" But Franca told Mary that she had already taken a room in a boarding house in the village and did not have the courage to break her lease so soon after engaging it. Mary told Franca not to worry. She would send Henry, her handyman, to help with Franca's belongings. That is what was done, and in that way Franca had come to Mary's house.

One night in her room, Mary said in confidence: "Franca, I am so proud of you. You are the only person recommended personally by Padre Pio, who said to me in confession: 'Maria, you must accept Franca as a member of your household.' " Thus Franca became the cook for Mary's household.

Franca considered Mary an "hourly person." Whatever Mary did, she did — or tried to do — on schedule. Sometimes, when Franca had finished her prayers in church, she would go up to Mary and say to her: "Mary, let's go home," whereupon Mary would reply sweetly: "Not yet. I must finish my prayers."

Finish? That was just Mary's way of speaking. She was never finished praying, for her prayers were a continuous union with God, even when they concerned seemingly ordinary, trivial matters. Mary Pyle, Franca said, used the books of daily meditation that were used by the Capuchin friars, such as *Thoughts and Affection on the Passion of Our Lord Jesus Christ* and *With St. Francis before God*. In addition, Mary possessed the pious, popular books on the Mass of St. Joseph, of the Madonna, of the Sacred Heart, of the deceased, and on the prayers to the Madonna of Pompei. Above all, she had books of prayers and liturgy: *The Seraphic Roman Breviary for Use by the Order of Friars Capuchin Minors; The Office of the Blessed Virgin Mary; The Missal*, in Latin and in English; *The Saint Andrew Missal; The Roman Parishioner*, which bore an autograph and the date December 5, 1917.

Mary had a briefcase in which she carried four prayer books and sometimes more when she went to church.

Mary Pyle as a Hostess

MARY Pyle was a charming, delightful hostess. She never exaggerated the importance of an event. Rather, she attempted to lighten a contradiction with a smile, with words of exhortation, sometimes begging her guests not to quarrel.

Mary would often entertain her guests with interesting accounts of her family and of her youth, of her experiences with Dr. Maria Montessori, with accounts of those who came to Padre Pio and had received spiritual, physical, and material help from him. An accomplished linguist, she was fluent in English, Italian, French, German, and Spanish and knew Latin to a considerable extent. Sometimes, because her guests were those who spoke only their native tongue, she conversed in Italian or English or German. One day she said to my sister: "I've become lost for a moment. In what language was I just speaking?"

At Mary's table every day for the noonday meal were the poor, members of society, professionals, artists, priests. One day at dinner, for example, Helena and I were introduced to the wife of the consolate of Malta; to a woman doctor who directed a large hospital in Ireland; to the famous singer from La Scala, Maria Marcucci; to the composer Frederico Caudana; and to the famous baritone Victor Damiani and his wife. All were guests at the table of Mary Pyle.

Dr. Maria Montessori

MARY Pyle, the daughter of an American millionaire, was related to the Rockefeller family. She often entertained her guests and members of her household (the women who lived and worked in her house were not called "servants" but "members of my household") with stories of her childhood or sometimes of her experiences with Dr. Maria Montessori, the noted educator of children.

According to Mary, when Doctor Montessori came to the United States for a visit, Mary went to the pier with a group of young women who had been Doctor Montessori's pupils in Rome, to meet the educator. Doctor Montessori greeted them warmly, then the reporters and local dignitaries who were also there. Soon she was taken to the Holland House, an elegant hotel in New York City.

There that afternoon, she was surrounded by staff, reporters, and photographers. Among those present were her American students who had met her at the dock. They had come to the hotel only to learn that they would not be able to see Doctor Monstessori in her suite. So many people had crowded into the hotel that the staff began turning away those without an appointment. To get past the staff, Mary Pyle said she and some of the others went out for dress and hat boxes. Then, pretending they were milliners and dressmakers making deliveries at the hotel, they managed to get past the hotel clerks, curious bystanders, and Doctor Montessori's staff and see her in her suite.

Padre Pio's Spiritual Children

I HAD first heard of Padre Pio's "Spiritual Children" through Mary Pyle. From his earliest years as a Franciscan friar, she said, Padre Pio's God-given gifts had enabled him to discern many of the sins of mankind, particularly of those whom he confessed. If a penitent inadvertently forgot to confess a grave fault, he was reminded of it, often in great detail. "I can see all of your life," he would say, "passing like a motion picture film." Over the years, he maintained a spiritual relationship with his Spiritual Children, guiding them to a fuller, more meaningful spirituality with our Lord and His Blessed Mother.

During his lifetime, Padre Pio accepted many people as his spiritual children. When he became aware of their goodwill, he would say to them: "I accept you, but don't disgrace me before God." He promised them that once they were lifted, he would not let them falter along the road of salvation.

In 1961, Padre Pio accepted as his Spiritual Children all the members of the Blue Army of Our Lady of Fatima. When the request to do so was made to him, Padre Pio replied; "Yes — if they behave!"

When I asked Mary Pyle what it meant to be a spiritual child of Padre Pio, she answered: "Padre Pio said, 'I will stand at the gates of Heaven and will not enter until all my Spiritual Children have entered'." Thus, my sister and I asked Padre Pio if we could become his spiritual children, and he said he would accept us.

Padre Pio's Prayer Groups

IT was said that all those who became a member of a Padre Pio prayer group automatically became his spiritual children. Even those who learned of Padre Pio's spiritual children applied at his monastery to become members of his spiritual family.

One day, Mary said, a spiritual son of Padre Pio said to him: "Padre Pio, I don't believe in hell." To which Padre Pio answered: "You will when you get there!" Another asked: "Padre Pio, should we tell white lies?" Padre Pio answered: "No, even if they don't harm anyone, they harm the soul. God is truth."

Another question asked him was: "In what way am I like God?" Padre Pio answered: "In the spirit for its faculties of intelligence, memory and will, which are not separate faculties, but together make up the soul."

It was through Mary Pyle that Helena and I learned how Padre Pio had formed prayer groups. Mary answered that the exact date was not precise but that in the 1940's Padre Pio had repeated the appeals of Pope Pius XII to the faithful to assemble at least once a month under the direction of a priest, having first obtained the permission of their local bishop to do so. They were to have no other obligation than to pray together.

From the beginning of his pontificate in 1939, Pope Pius XII, himself a deeply spiritual man, showed benevolence toward Padre Pio. The accounts of the miracles of Padre Pio would leave His Holiness in deep thought.

Little by little, Padre Pio's spiritual children gathered in their villages and towns and formed prayer groups for the purpose of praying together. With no central organization or direction, the groups spread throughout Italy and abroad. In 1949, the Casa Sollievo della Sofferenza (Home for the Relief of Suffering) began to provide information about the prayer groups in newspapers, publishing the days and times of meetings (usually once a month). At the same time, the Home distributed some rules, so that everything would take place with ecclesiastical discipline, saying the meetings must be organized with the permission of the local bishop and must be directed by a priest.

Padre Pio said that all members of his prayer groups, present and future, were his spiritual children. He followed the work of the group leaders and on occasion advised them. The groups stand as a monument to his mission. Today there are more than 2,000 Padre Pio groups scattered around the world.

The Capuchin Monastery and Emanuele Brunatto

MARY Pyle told us the following story about the building of the Capuchin monastery and church in Padre Pio's hometown of Pietrelcina, about how she had accepted the invitation to do the work, and about the assistance she received from Emanuele Brunatto. One day, she said, a group of citizens from Pietrelcina asked her if she would build a monastery for the Capuchin Fathers of the province in their small town. The project seemed worthwhile, but, she told the delegation of citizens, she would not think of consenting without first asking Padre Pio what he thought about the proposal. When she did so, Padre Pio smiled benevolently and said: "Yes. Do it quickly. Let it be dedicated to the Holy Family."

Although Mary had received Padre Pio's approval of the project, in which were to be combined a church and the Seraphic Seminary, other events — most notably World War II — interfered. As sometimes happens, certain difficulties arose that made it necessary to stop construction of the church and

Mary Pyle: Under the Spiritual Guidance of Padre Pio   31

monastery. Supported by Padre Pio, though, Mary Pyle wasn't discouraged. Not only that, when funds were depleted Mary made available her personal funds. During the war, the still unfinished structure was occupied by German troops. Eventually, through Mary Pyle's zeal, generosity, and faith, the church and seminary were completed.

She was assisted in the building by the architect Emanuele Brunatto, about whom she told Helena and me the following story.

Emanuele, born in Torino, Italy, in 1892, became a wealthy man. For some forty years he battled for the cause of Padre Pio, perhaps because he recognized the latter's greatness. He himself went before some of the most important cardinals and showed them papers detailing infamous accusations made by enemies of Padre Pio. He wanted to go even further, to take the matter before the United Nations.

As a young man, Emanuele Brunatto had lived the life of a libertine. He thought of virtually everything but God. Then, at the age of thirty, all that ended. Emanuele became possessed of a mystical desire to say good-bye to his previous life, good-bye to romance, fine foods, elegant fashions. He disappeared and went to live as a hermit.

He had learned that in the mountains of the Gargano lived a monk named Padre Pio, who bore the Stigmata and who had unusual powers. With the same impetuousness that had made him give up his philandering earlier life, Emanuele attached himself to Padre Pio and became his ardent follower. For three years he lived in a tumbledown shack, a refuge to stray chickens next door to the monastery. His greatest joy came from the fleeting moments he spent near or with Padre Pio.

In the early 1920s, Padre Pio often was severely criticized by powerful figures within the Church. At the center of the struggle was Pasquale Gagliardi, the archbishop of Manfredonia. In defense of Padre Pio, and to the mockery of various priests, Emanuele presented to ten cardinals at the Vatican a detailed report of corruption, of revenge and envy on the part of Padre Pio's enemies. In his report, he included a profile of his own life. The cardinals asked, "Who is this? An angel with his lightning sword revenging offenses against God, or a demon intent on overthrowing all?" Monsignor Bevilacqua arrived from Rome to assess the situation firsthand. After his inspection, Padre Pio's lot improved.

Emanuele Brunatto had the Midas touch; everything he touched seemed to turn to gold. Soon after the dispute with the cardinals at the Vatican, he left Italy and went to France where he became a financier and gained control of the French railway system. With his wealth, however, he returned to his old ways, to the Brunatto who loved women, fine foods, and elegant fashions. This time, though, there was a restlessness within him. He continued to be in church every morning. Then, one day, he decided to send a large check to San Giovanni Rotondo, a town never far from his thoughts. His charity took numerous forms. During World War II, in Paris, he organized "Hot Drinks," places where those who had little or nothing to eat could go. He searched for the widows and orphans of fallen Italians who were still living in France, and provided for those he found. He organized trains for the sick and financed trips to Lourdes for those seeking cures.

Emanuele Brunatto, during World War II, was involved in a case having to do with allegations of collaborating with the Nazis. Who could help him? He was advised to see the new apostolic delegate sent to France by Pope Pius XII, partly to placate President de Gaulle, who wanted to banish from France each and every bishop who had collaborated — or was thought to have collaborated with — the Germans. Mostly, however, the apostolic delegate was sent because he was a humanistic priest. The delegate, Angelo Roncalli, spoke French poorly, with the accent of his native Bergamo; nevertheless, he made himself understood. Emanuele presented himself and, much to his surprise, became Roncalli's friend. Emanuele later recounted to the apostolic delegate how, during the war, he had helped save sixteen thousand

Jews, and of his generosity to the Church. He expanded on the great years of his stay in San Giovanni Rotondo. The future Pope John XXIII listened, adjusted his cap, and smiled.

After the war, Emanuele Brunatto returned to Italy, to aid Mary Pyle in building the church and seminary. During the construction he served not only as supervisor but as bookkeeper for the project. Construction of the monastery was accomplished in three years, but as of 1930 the church remained unfinished, due to lack of funds, and was not resumed until 1949. With the completion of the monastery in Pietrelcina, though, the home longed for by the Capuchins became a reality. Now, Emanuele Brunatto hoped, Padre Pio could return to his native land.

Enjoying the confidence and trust of Padre Pio, Brunatto applied his considerable intellectual abilities and organizational skills to the project. At one point, he formed a committee of citizens who, despite their divided interests and political bickering, were fond of Padre Pio and held him in high esteem. It was through Brunatto's tenacity and influence that the acquisition of land in the countryside, for the monastery and church, as well as the license from the Civil Authority to begin construction, were obtained. Overcoming these difficulties, he had the pleasure of seeing the cornerstone for the monastery laid by Archbishop Salvatore Pannulla on June 13, 1926.

Two decades later, in 1947, Bishop Luigi Lavitrana, Cardinal Prefect for Religious Affairs, gave approval for the Capuchins to move to Pietrelcina.

While living in Pietrelcina, Brunatto was the guest of Padre Pio's parents, in Vico Storta Valle (street of the crooked valley) in a small room where Padre Pio as a child had studied. For Christmas 1925, he made a manger and installed it in the mother church. Then, on Holy Thursday 1926, he prepared a sepulchre.

In wintertime, Emanuele Brunatto was the only one in the village who wore an overcoat. The gentlemen of Pietrelcina wore cloaks. He was conscientious about attending holy Mass and other church functions, and devotedly assisted in the services. He was faithful in receiving the sacrament of Holy Communion (the men in Pietrelcina received communion only at Easter and on rare occasions, such as confirmation and weddings. In Pietrelcina, he was both popular and respected, exhibiting courtesy toward everyone and avoiding gossip.

For months, Mary said, they worked hard. When they encountered a snag and needed Padre Pio's advice, Mary would get in touch with him through his father. Emanuele Brunatto was untiring in working on the project and was a wise collaborator.

When they had completed all the work they could, Mary decided it was time to return to San Giovanni Rotondo. Emanuele Brunatto offered to drive her home, and she accepted his invitation. They left Pietrelcina and drove for about three hours, until they reached Foggia, a town about twenty-four miles short of their destination. Emanuele drove up to a hotel and stopped. "I cannot drive any farther," he said. "I am exhausted. Let's stop at this hotel and get some rest." Mary admitted that she too was tired; so they went in and Emanuele booked rooms for them.

When they reached their rooms, Emanuele insisted that Mary lie down and rest. For some reason, however, she did not, and instead sat in a chair, all the while wondering about Emanuele's insistence that she lie down on the couch and rest. Suddenly she smelled roses, violets, and lilies. It was an aroma that she associated with Padre Pio. "Emanuele, do you have something that belongs to Padre Pio?"

"Yes," he replied; "in that suitcase are some old vestments of Padre Pio's that he wore in Pietrelcina. The monks gave them to me."

Mary went over to the luggage to verify this. It was true; she could detect the sweet odor so characteristic of the clothing Padre Pio wore. Suddenly realizing that he must be trying to convey a message to her, she informed Emanuele that she could stay no longer at the hotel, that she wished to go to San Giovanni Rotondo immediately. Although he was stunned at this sudden change of plans, especially since only a few minutes earlier Mary had said she was extremely tired, they checked out of the hotel and continued on their way.

Mary Pyle concluded her reminiscene of Emanuele Brunatto by asking us to pray that he would die like a martyr, so the Blessed Mother could help save his soul.

Pietrelcina

MARY Pyle was the major force behind the building of a church and seminary for the Capuchin friars at Pietrelcina, the small town where Padre Pio was born. The construction was aided financially by generous donations from the villagers and others, as well as from families that had emigrated to the United States from the town. The friary had been completed, awaiting only the arrival of the occupants, when World War II engulfed Italy. Due to occupation by invading armies and the great damage that ensued, the Capuchins were not able to take possession of the seminary until 1947.

The adjoining church, built later, was dedicated to the Holy Family. Mary Pyle, together with a contingent from San Giovanni Rotondo, attended the consecration ceremonies held on May 19, 1951.

Since that time, a monumental altar has been added, built with contributions from benefactors. Thus was fulfilled a prophecy made by the young seminarian Padre Pio years earlier, when, because of poor health, he lived in Pietrelcina with his family. One day during that period, while on an evening walk with the parish priest, Don Salvatore Pannullo, Padre Pio stopped suddenly and, looking in the direction of the church and monastery, said: "I smell incense. I hear the chant of friars rising before the throne of God."

As recently as 1962, as further improvements were being made to the church, an earthquake shook the town; but the church and the friary were damaged only slightly. Five years later, as a token of gratitude for the Capuchins' work among the people, a street was named for them. Then, in 1971, a striking monument to Padre Pio was erected in the front garden to the friary, and a bust of Mary Pyle was placed at the entrance to the seminary.

The Early Years

BORN in Morristown, New Jersey, April 17, 1888, to James Tolman Pyle and Adelaide McAlpine Pyle, Mary was christened Adelia in the local Presbyterian church, where her parents were members (they were faithful Presbyterians from New England, and raised Mary [then Adelia] in the teachings and precepts of the Presbyterian church). She had two older brothers, James and David, a younger sister, Sara, and two younger brothers, Charles and Gordon. Her maternal grandparents, a family of Scotch-Irish origin, owned the McAlpine Hotel in New York City. Mary's Uncle Charles had married Mary Rockefeller, of New York's Rockefeller family. James Pyle made a fortune selling soap, and Mary remembered the product's advertising slogan: "Pyle's Bubbles."

Her family lived comfortably — perhaps, she sometimes wondered, "too comfortably." For instance, at home she wasn't allowed even to light a match; everything must be done by a maid or a butler, and there usually were about eight servants at the family's beck and call.

Mary maintained that she was more content with her life in

San Giovanni Rotondo. She felt free of her former way of life, which she regarded as a way of life resembling slavery or at least servitude of some sort. "In everything, I prefer the simple way of life I now lead," she said, "even in something as ordinary as eating."

Her mother had come to San Giovanni Rotondo and, later, her sister-in-law, Zene, who was a Catholic and was married to Mary's tall, handsome brother, Gordon. Gordon used to visit Manfredonia in a yacht, which he very much wanted Padre Pio to bless. On one such visit, because it was Padre Pio's policy never to leave the monastery, Father Raffaele and Father Vittore went to bless the craft, at anchor in the Gulf of Manfredonia. Although Mary's other brothers — James, David, and Charles — came to meet Padre Pio, Gordon and Zene visited him more often. Gordon wanted to become a Catholic and he studied and read numerous books as preparation for baptism. He was forced to give up the project, however, when he became ill.

The last time Mary's mother visited Padre Pio, she talked to him, with Mary, as usual, translating. As Mrs. Pyle rose to leave, Padre Pio remarked: "Let us hope we will see each other again," adding while pointing his finger heavenward, "if not here, then up there!"

Mary was educated primarily through private tutors and, later, at the Chapin School in Princeton, New Jersey, and the Masters School in Dobbs Ferry, New York. When her parents thought it time for her to study a particular foreign language, a private tutor for the language chosen came to live with the family and instruct Mary. From such an intensive course (she spoke only the language being studied), Mary learned to read and speak French, German, Italian, and Spanish correctly and fluently. At the Chapin School and then the Masters School, she studied English and Latin, as well as music, dance, voice, and pedagogy (as the art or science of teaching was then called).

As a young woman, Mary (or Adelia), along with her family,

attended dances in New York City. In addition, she enjoyed horseback-riding but had once been hurt in a riding accident and thus had to give up the sport. Often in later years, when her feet hurt, Mary would say it was the price she had to pay for all that dancing she had done in her youth.

Mary, though still young, felt that she was old enough to make up her own mind in such matters and, because she was determined to become a Catholic, sought to convince her family — especially her parents — of her determination. Meanwhile, her father and mother, in an effort to dissuade her, invited a succession of clergymen and laymen prominent in the Presbyterian church to their home, to talk to Adelia and, they hoped, induce her to change her mind. Thus, the head pastor of the church in Morristown arrived one day, and he and Adelia talked about her plans for converting. At one point in their discussion, she asked: "Do *you* believe in your religion? Truly believe? Are you entirely convinced that Presbyterianism is the right religion for you?"

After a moment's hesitation, the minister replied: "To tell the truth — no."

"Then why do you wish me to continue being a Presbyterian, and not become a Catholic, as I wish to do?"

After a few more such episodes, her parents dropped the matter, leaving their daughter to set her own course in the matter of religion.

In the matter of matrimony — or, specially, making a proper marriage — Mr. and Mrs. Pyle maintained an active interest. One well-to-do young man in whom she was interested was rebuffed when he committed the gaffe of coming to visit Adelia while she was alone at the family's estate in the country. Then, shortly after World War I, she fell in love with a man her own age; but her parents were not pleased with him and, instead, proposed sending Adelia to Italy to study. After all, they argued, Adelia had already demonstrated an aptitude for languages: Italy seemed an ideal place to further her study.

Thus Adelia sailed for Europe, settling in Rome, where she met the famous educator Maria Montessori and, through the latter's influence, began her study of pedagogy. The suitor she had left behind continued to write to her, however, and because of that her mood grew darker rather than lighter. Eventually, though, involvement in study, together with the simple passage of time, worked to heal her loneliness and broken heart.

Sometime later, Doctor Montessori received an invitation to lecture in the United States on her methods. When she and her protege arrived in New York, each went her own way. Doctor Montessori had long been aware that Adelia spoke five languages, a fact she mentally filed away for future use. Later, when it was time to return to Rome, Doctor Montessori contacted Adelia and asked if she would like to accompany her as an interpreter of Doctor Montessori's method of teaching. Adelia's brother, James, urged her to go, saying "It's for a good cause." Adelia thought about the offer briefly, then decided to accept it. She wrote to her mother, who was traveling in California (her father had by then died). Mrs. Pyle responded quickly — though not quickly enough. "Do not accept the position," she wrote. "The work and travel will take you away from home too often and for too long." The letter arrived too late: Adelia had meanwhile made up her mind and had departed.

Adelia traveled with Doctor Montessori through various European cities and to several countries, interpreting the Montessori lectures in English, French, German, Italian, and Spanish. The system espoused by the educator offered a program of reform, a new kind of educational institution, one which, it was claimed, could achieve significant results in a remarkably short time. A new generation of children would be trained to be independent, productive members of society. At the same time, numerous problems of the day would be solved. Educators, legislators, physicians, writers, parents — everyone was fascinated by Doctor Montessori's Casa dei Bambini (House of Children) in Rome. Many came to see for themselves and, when they left, spread the word about what they had seen and learned.

Adelia served as Doctor Montessori's interpreter for ten years. Of great importance, the travel gave her an opportunity to study closely the Catholic faith, to which she had felt drawn for some time. In her travels and association with Doctor Montessori, Adelia was irresistibly attracted to Catholicism. At the same time, she was impressed and spiritually edified by Doctor Montessori's example, by the respect people in all walks of life exhibited toward the educator. For example, Doctor Montessori's black wardrobe mistress accompanied her employer on lecture tours, for meetings and social engagements. On one occasion, unhappy with the condition of a suit of clothes, Doctor Montessori scolded the girl. When the girl burst into tears, the professor took her hand and kissed it! This humility impressed Adelia. "Only a person of deep religious conviction would do such a thing," she later commented.

During one Holy Week, Adelia and Doctor Montessori went to Rome, and Adelia accompanied the educator to various Catholic functions held that week. Later, she visited the cathedral and Marian shrines of Germany, France, and Spain. Above all the rest, she preferred the sanctuary of the Madonna of Montserrat, where every day she went to pray before the image of the Virgin. It was in this sanctuary that Adelia Pyle made her decision to become a Catholic. Later Mary told us that, at the solemn moment in the Mass when the host is elevated for adoration, she would say: "Jesus, if you are present in the host, give me the faith to believe it!"

In 1913, after preparation and instruction under a Jesuit priest, Adelia, dressed all in white, was baptized and took the name Mary. She was twenty-five years of age. Later, she told friends that she had asked that a Capuchin priest perform the baptismal ceremonies. She did not remember a particular reason for the request other than the fact that in Spain a Capuchin priest frequently had come to see Doctor Montessori. In reply, the Jesuit priest to whom she made the request said it mattered little who performed the ceremony; what matterd was that she receive the sacrament of baptism in the rites of the Catholic church.

The news of Mary's conversion greatly disturbed her family in New York City, especially her mother, who had her will rewritten to exclude her daughter from an inheritance. Her daughter — now *Mary* Pyle — accepted the disinheritance with composure, keeping her sorrow to herself. Her grief wasn't so much over the loss of the inheritance as it was over her mother's aloofness and coolness. Her mother seemed little interested in hearing her daughter's viewpoint on the matter. Meanwhile, as a means of earning a living, Mary continued to work with Doctor Montessori.

A few years after these events took place, Padre Pio, an obscure Capuchin friar, received the visible Stigmata on his hands, feet, and side and thus became the first stigmatized priest in the history of the Roman Catholic Church and to be called a modern Saint Francis.

In her memoirs, Mary Pyle writes that it was about 1921, while she was in London with Maria Montessori to translate into English a course on the educator's method of educating children, that Mary first heard of Padre Pio and his Stigmata. She soon believed in the Italian friar but did not at that time wish to see him, believing that to do so would be merely out of curiosity. In the meantime, she maintained that belief was enough.

While in London, Mary found a small book on the human will which she liked very much. Written by a Father Caussade, *The Surrender of the Will to God*, translated from the French, was in an abridged edition; so she searched until she found the unabridged, original edition. This edition had been issued in two volumes — the first entirely devoted to the subject of the surrender of the will to God, the second containing letters written by Father Caussade to his spiritual daughters in an enclosed convent. Mary's reading of the book convinced her that she needed a spiritual mentor like

Father Caussade, and thus she began to say the Novena to Our Lady of Pompei.

From London, Mary went to Rome. There, she went each day to the Church of the Holy Name of Jesus. She also prayed to Our Lady of the Street that, God willing, she would find such a spiritual mentor.

In the summer of 1923, Doctor Montessori and Mary went to the Isle of Capri, where they established residence. They would remain there until the early autumn. Rina Caterinici d'Ergin, a dear friend of Mary's, both having been pupils of Doctor Montessori in Rome and a Romanian of the Orthodox faith, visited her at Capri. Rina told Mary that she would like to meet Padre Pio, the Stigmatist. She wanted to ask him if it was the will of God that she become a Catholic. "But of course," Mary replied; "he is a Catholic, so he will say 'yes'." But Rina dismissed this reasoning. "I want to hear it from his own lips," she said. "I won't see him unless you come with me." Finally, Mary agreed to accompany Rina to meet Padre Pio.

They left Capri on October 2, 1923 and spent the night in Naples. From there they went to Foggia by train, then to San Giovanni Rotondo on a bus that shuttled daily between Foggia and San Giovanni Rotondo. In those days there were no large, roomy buses such as we have today. Instead, Mary and Rina rode in a cramped rundown bus that shuddered so badly and made so much noise that it constantly seemed about to break apart.

On the brisk autumn morning of October 3, 1923, the bus arrived in San Giovanni Rotondo. It stopped in the square before the monastery church. As often happened, a group of peasants were there, observing the comings and goings of the travelers. This time, the travelers getting off were Mary Pyle and Rina d'Ergin. The blond, elegantly dressed Mary asked one of the onlookers where they could find Padre Pio.

A peasant woman offered to show them to the monastery. On the way, Rina and Mary were struck by the condition of the area, especially the delapidated buildings. Soon they reached the small, seventeenth-century church that was part of the monastery. Placing scarfs on their heads, they entered it.

At first, because the interior was dimly lit, the church seemed deserted. Then they noticed the solitary figure of a monk, in an alcove set at an angle under the main altar. The monk was praying. They could see that his hands were bandaged. The woman who was their guide went up to the monk. When she was quite close, she said, "Padre Pio," then, louder: "Padre Pio!" Still, the monk did not respond; he did not move even slightly. With his eyes fixed on the Crucifix, he continued with his praying. Taking courage, the woman touched him on the shoulder. At this, he turned abruptly and, in a reproachful tone, said: "What is it you wish with me? Can't you see that I am praying? Let me continue to do so — in peace with the Lord!"

On this occasion, as it turned out, Rina and Mary were not to meet the monk with the Stigmata. Nevertheless, this brief encounter with Padre Pio struck something deep inside Mary. This, her first encounter with the friar, was one that would alter the course of her life. She looked past Padre Pio's brusque manner, discerning a manner that concealed an inestimable goodness. It was a goodness that would soon conquer her spirit.

On October 4, 1923, when she met Padre Pio, Mary Pyle was an attractive, thirty-five-year-old woman in the prime of life, tall and sophisticated. In later years, all she said about the meeting was that their "eyes met, and I knelt at his feet and said, 'Padre'. He put his stigmatized hands on my head and said, 'My daughter, do not travel anymore. Remain here.' "

Mary and her friend Rina returned to Capri, where Mary continued her work as an interpreter for Doctor Montessori. Sometime later, she went with Doctor Montessori to London and then to Amsterdam. Now that she had met Padre Pio, however, her life seemed different; she had become restless, dissatisfied with her life in a vague, undefined way. She was no longer at peace; she would often visualize Padre Pio raising a bleeding hand in benediction.

One day during the trip, Mary said to her friend and employer: "There is a saint living in this world, and I regret not being able to be near him. I wish to return to see him, and I would like you to accompany me." Doctor Montessori readily consented to go with Mary.

As has been mentioned, in later years, Mary frequently spoke of events that occurred in her youth and of her work and travel with Maria Montessori. Once she recounted a dream she had during that period. In her dream, Mary was riding in a stagecoach with Doctor Montessori. The horses were galloping furiously across a boundless plain. The coach reached a crossroads, and someone mysteriously appeared who seemed to be an official with considerable authority. With great courage, the figure seized the horses' reins and brought them to a stop. Suddenly, to the right of the coach, there opened a road that had previously not been apparent. The figure spoke for the first time: "Blessed are those who take the right road, for they will be saved!" At that point, the dream ended.

Mary Pyle had since forgotten about the dream. When she and Doctor Montessori reached San Giovanni Rotondo, however, she went to the sacristy to greet Padre Pio, and they talked. During their conversation, Padre Pio startled Mary by saying: "I will put a chain around you and I will bridle you!" At the moment Padre Pio spoke these words, something in Mary's mind revived the dream about the stagecoach out of control and the mysterious figure who stopped it. Immediately she said: "Padre, I would like to tell you something. I want you to hear about a dream I had." Padre Pio made a small motion indicating that he was listening, and Mary told him about the dream.

When she had finished, Padre Pio smiled and said: "Remain here!" Mary took this to mean that she was to leave her current employment and settle in San Giovanni Rotondo. She told Padre Pio of her desire to do this. Even though she had not mentioned to him that her mother had all along opposed her working for Doctor Montessori, he said to her: "Obey your mother!" From his words,

Mary took courage. She glanced at her friend and employer for approval, and Doctor Montessori nodded, saying: "If that is what you wish, what else is there to do? What else can I say?"

With the matter thus settled, it was time for Doctor Montessori to leave. She assumed that Mary would return with her to Rome to collect her belongings. The bus arrived, and as they were about to board it, Doctor Montessori turned to Mary and said: "Hurry and get it!" Disconcerted, Mary stammered: "I can't. I can't. I feel paralized, as though someone had nailed my feet to the ground."

Doctor Montessori did not press the matter. She boarded the bus alone, which left without Mary, who remained behind. They were not to meet again. Only after the bus had been gone several minutes was Mary able to bestir herself and decided what to do next. The first thing to be done, she decided, was find a place to stay.

In later years, Mary said, when Doctor Montessori greeted close friends in Foggia, she expressed annoyance with Padre Pio, claiming that he had caused her to "lose" her valued friend and interpreter, Mary Pyle.

The Decision to Remain near Padre Pio

IN the 1920's the environs of the monastery of Saint Mary of the Graces resembled a desert, it was so barren. The monastery was connected to San Giovanni Rotondo by a narrow, poorly maintained road used by the occasional cart and by peasants going to gather firewood or by shepherds taking their flocks into the mountains to graze.

After a short period of searching, Mary found lodging with a family named Vinciguerra. From their house she would walk the long, difficult road to the monastery in all kinds of weather. She especially wanted to attend the Mass Padre Pio then celebrated at seven in the morning. To avoid having to walk back and forth to the village, she would bring her lunch in a bag. At noon, like the other pilgrims, Mary sat in front of the monastery on a stone wall beneath an elm and ate her lunch.

Mary awaited her turn for confession to Padre Pio. When she confessed, she asked him what she should do now that she had taken up residence in San Giovanni Rotondo. "Build a good house for yourself and for others," Padre Pio advised her, "because here will remain the imprint of your work." So Mary began to search for an architect to design a house for her, and inquired in the village about hiring one. Upon finding a suitable architect, she asked Padre Pio for his advice concerning the location of the house. He suggested that she build it on land to the right of the monastery (when one faces the structure), which today is owned by the Serritelli sisters. Mary replied that the location would give her no privacy. She thought the bottom of the hill on which the monastery stood would be better. "If that is what you wish, go ahead," Padre Pio said.

Mary later regretted her choice of location. Those who have been there need no explanation why she felt this way; they know all too well how difficult it was for Mary, in the last years of her life, to climb the steep hill to the church. To make matters worse, a strong wind usually blows from the Adriatic. Mary even had an iron handrail installed in the wall that ran alongside the road. She wanted nothing to deprive her of attendance at Mass each day. Only after Padre Pio told her that, due to her health, she was not to attend Mass every day did she stop — but by then she did not have long to live.

While her house was under construction, Mary began the work that remains today as a monument to her charity. She met young people and invited the neediest among them to her quarters, where she taught them their catechism. When parents could not

Mary Pyle: Under the Spiritual Guidance of Padre Pio 47

afford it, Mary provided the youngsters with the proper clothes for their first Holy Communion. If mealtime overlapped, she gave them a light meal before they left. Thus began, said Peter Cugino (one of those befriended by Mary), a friendship that over the years grew and grew.

Eleven months after her arrival in San Giovanni Rotondo, Mary Pyle wrote in her notebook:

> *August 22, 1924. "Behold we here have a heart full of joy and peace. . . . Here, in this calm beside Padre Pio, one understands things better, even the beauty of our work. I do not speak with Padre Pio, only in passing, when I kiss his hand and receive a blessing; but for me his presence teaches more than a library full of books."*

Mary's house became an extension of the monastery. It was, in effect, a small monastery of religious women who collaborated with their brother monks, studying the chants for the Mass and for other functions, even to the extent of stamping envelopes for the monastery's correspondence. The house, together with its owner, Mary Pyle, became a "little house of charity" where souls in need of peace, the love of God, and prayer found hospitality.

Mary became a teacher of young girls, helping them with their singing and with the formation of their spiritual lives. She worked with the Franciscan movement and collaborated with Padre Pio and other Capuchin fathers. Officially she was delegated to the direction and assistance of the Third Order Franciscans, foreign missions, and vocations.

Mary spent her first Christmas in San Giovanni Rotondo that year of 1923. From her room in the home of Calogero Vinciguerra, every morning she walked the two miles to the monastery. On Christmas morning, Don Giovanni, the father of the Serritelli sisters, went to the monastery to offer best wishes to Padre Pio. In his characteristic manner, Padre Pio asked a question that was at the same time a suggestion: "Why don't you have Miss Mary Pyle come to your house and spend Christmas with your family?" Gladly Don Giovanni replied that he would indeed invite her. And thus Mary was accepted in the home of the Serritellis and there spent Christmas. There was joy and harmony in that family that Christmas Day. Before the meal everyone joined in saying grace and Don Giovanni blessed the food.

Mary soon received marvelous proof of the kindness the Serritelli family had shown her that Christmas. Sometime later, Don Giovanni became seriously ill. Every day, before walking to the monastery, Mary came out of her hotel and went to the Serritellis' house for a visit with the ailing Don Giovanni. She was thus able to give a daily account to Padre Pio of the sick man's condition. Then on December 3, 1927, Don Giovanni died. The death of her husband caused his widow, Maria Michela, to go into shock, where she remained for some time. Living in the house where everything reminded her of her husband was to continually suffer, and before long the widow herself became gravely ill.

Mary's house was finished at that time, and she and a small staff moved in. Padre Pio desired that Signora Serritelli go to live in Mary Pyle's house. There she should be able to gain some relief from her ailment. In addition, she would be distracted by other occupations which might possibly lessen her sorrow. Padre Pio suggested that her daughter, Elvira, go with her mother to Mary's house, to look after her mother. It was thus arranged that Elvira and her mother would live in Mary's house.

The ailing widow, with the faithful attention of Mary Pyle and the others, improved noticeably, to the point where it was decided that she should return to her own house. As soon as she did that, however, she became ill again, and asked to return to Mary's house near the monastery. It was then that the Serritelli sisters decided to build their own house near the monastery, and in fact quickly acquired a piece of land, along with the rural house that belonged to Joseph Ercolino.

Mary occasionally talked about the "Schola Cantorum" (School of Song), the all-girl choir she rehearsed and conducted and for which she played the organ. The choir sang hymns and otherwise accompanied the Masses in the monastery church. (Years earlier, in her home in the United States, Mary had had at her disposal three concert pianos; but she didn't want to study piano, only singing, because she had been told that she had a good voice. She liked to dance, to read poetry, and she frequented the theater, where she listened to the performances of the best artists and attended some brilliant plays. She related this background mostly to entertain her guests.)

Not content with being a practicing Catholic leading a pious life and doing good works for the common good of the faithful, Mary wished also to ascend to the life of evangelical perfection in the footsteps of her spiritual director. She asked Padre Pio one day if she should become a nun in some Franciscan institution, and he answered: "The convent is not for you. Enroll in the Franciscan Third Order" (an organization for laypersons).

Mary followed his suggestion. She considered the suggestion more a command (as she considered all his answers to questions), and formally submitted a request to the superior of the monastery, asking to dress in the "habit of penance." (The habit may not be worn daily by Third Order members, only by permission, and is permitted to be used for burial.) Permission was granted to Mary to wear the habit daily. And, thus, on August 24, 1924, Padre Pio blessed the habit Mary would wear. A year after termination of the novitiate, on September 6, 1925, she received the holy profession from Padre Pio, as well as the religious name Sister Pia.

Mary decided to consecrate herself totally to the Lord with the vows of chastity and obedience. For the love of the poverty of Christ and under the example of Saint Francis of Assisi, she embraced poverty, took off all her rich secular clothes, and dressed in the coarse Franciscan habit consisting of a brown tunic with a white cord hanging at her side and an attached rosary and sandals. She pledged unconditional obedience to her spiritual director, Padre Pio. Afterward, she said, "When I adopted the Franciscan habit, I definitely cut the bridge between myself and the world."

For August 27, 1924, she wrote in her notebook:

> *"Today has been another day filled with beauty. Perhaps there is no other day more peaceful and intimate as Sunday, above all, in the afternoon when the Rosary is said together with Padre Pio, and he is kneeling in front of the altar on a small pillow, with his arms resting on a chair, and (he is) reading certain prayers from his Missal, and then together singing the Litany of the Madonna and then his giving the benediction. Afterwards he turned simply and called me or rather he made a sign for me to come and place myself at the small step of the altar, where, repeating word for word, he asked the question whether I wished to accept the habit of the Third Order of the Franciscans. When I said "I do," he placed the habit on me and gave me the cord to put on myself. Then, in the sacristy, he wrote the name that I had chosen — Sister Pia. This little book is a real treasure; no one is permitted to write in it, only the Father Director of the Congregation. All those, like him, become Third Order Franciscans, and he is always so pleased!*
>
> *Everything is so extraordinary in this mystical corner of the world, in this school for souls, where the healer, teacher and father, Padre Pio, is preparing a net of souls in order to encircle the entire world, fishing for souls for Jesus. He calls them forth with his vibrant voice and with his suffering and . . . wounds. He calls them with the waves of his perfume, or that of various flowers . . . How lucky for me to have met with the greatest saint since Saint Francis."*

Becoming a Member of the Third Order Franciscans

MARY Pyle became a member of the Third Order Franciscans, with special permission to wear the brown habit daily. She had a rosary at her side and sandals on her feet, and in appearance she resembled the Capuchin friars. She not only wore the habit of the Franciscan Capuchins, she adopted their prayer life, reading the Divine Office as they did. In her house, the rose-colored building among the almond trees that resembled a small castle, was the first house to break the absolute sense of the desert that existed at that time.

One day, Mary's mother received a long letter from San Giovanni Rotondo, which read:

> *"My dear parents, I am really happy. I have found living in this deserted place, (in) an enchanting wheat-filled country, that there is another life, (one) that is worth living without care or preoccupation. I have found that more than the flesh must be fed; the spirit must also be fed, and nothing feeds the spirit more than prayer.*
>
> *There lives here in a cold and small monastery a competitor of St. Francis of Assisi, who is named Padre Pio, and his hands and feet are pierced by the Stigmata. Every morning he celebrates Mass before sunrise, when the peasants begin to go to work in the fields. All his daily life is an example of humility and dedication to his Lord, He scorns worldly goods and considers supreme only the love (of) Christ. I feel as if I have always been here, among these people; it seems (that) I was born here. Only the homesickness for you affects my heart; but I pray always for you. Of all the things that belong to me, I do not know what to*

do; all I want to do is to help those who suffer, those who hunger and those who are unclothed."

Mary's mother, now in despair, rushed to San Giovanni Rotondo, hoping to persuade her daughter to return to the United States. But her efforts were futile. The daughter of the "Soap King of New York" had chosen to live near Padre Pio and to live in charity. The anxiety of Mary's early days in her new life was relieved when help from her family in the United States began to arrive. The family began sending part of the family income to her, much of which she turned over to those in need.

Mary Pyle Settles in San Giovanni Rotondo

WHEN Mary was settled in San Giovanni Rotondo, her mother — having given up her attempts to get Mary to return home — gave Mary a parlor set, one not luxurious but simple, that would correspond to the Franciscan way of life Mary had embraced. Whenever Adelaide Pyle visited her daughter, Mary would arrange a meeting between her mother and Padre Pio. She hoped that her mother would also embrace the Catholic religion; but, to Padre Pio, Adelaide said: "For my religion, I would be burned alive!" Later, when Mary, still hoping her mother would convert, spoke to Padre Pio about the matter, he replied: "Let us not confuse ideas. She will be saved because she is in good faith."

On another occasion, Adelaide Pyle told her daughter: "How I would like to kneel in Padre Pio's confession and confess to him. But I cannot speak Italian." When he heard this remark, Padre Pio said: "Would that she had done that — because I would have known what to do about the language."

Mary's brother, James, wrote, saying that in New York City

they sometimes had guests who, unaware of the name she took when she converted, inquired about "Adelia," to which Mrs. Pyle quickly answered: "She is on a mountain in Italy, in order to become a saint!"

One day Padre Pio said to Mary: "We are in need of an organist. There is an old organ in our church. Do you think you could play it?"

"I am pleased to learn to play the organ, in order to serve the Lord all the more," she replied. Thus Mary Pyle became Padre Pio's organist. Later, after she had become a Third Order Franciscan and acquired the old pump organ, Mary regretted not having learned to play earlier. Nonetheless, she began to study the organ. Her goal was to play and direct the Schola Cantorum during services at the church. At about this time, someone arrived in San Giovanni Rotondo who played the organ well enough to teach Mary to play. Through Elena Bandini, she learned to play well. When Elena later became ill, Mary continued to play the organ at daily functions; but for large church events, such as religious feasts, Rina Santovito, a concert pianist from central Italy, played the organ and directed the choir.

Mary told me once that she had used a table knife to beat time when accompanying the singers. Rehearsals were held in the dining room of her house. Laughing, she recalled how good and intelligent the members of the congregation were, and how surprised she had been at the results: many in the congregation had praised both the singing and Mary's performance at the organ. In fact, recordings were made of performances of the choir, with Mary at the organ, that were sold in shops offering religious goods. (Actually, *schola cantorum* is song in thanksgiving to the Lord. The entire project had come about because of Padre Pio's desire that religious functions be conducted with decorum and honor.)

Conversations with Padre Pio

IN the early years, Mary Pyle was one of the few women with whom Padre Pio would stop and converse. He often spoke of the bitterness that had been caused by his being severe, and even crabby, with some of the local women, confiding to Mary that some of the women, in their eagerness to touch him, had in times past crowded around, jumping excitedly and squeezing his hands and arms. He was bewildered by this behavior and had had to be severe with the women. "I don't like to be that way," he said, "but if I didn't, they would have smothered me!"

"Those women," Mary told me once, "do not for a moment speak of grace or of miracles. Their faith is so deep-rooted that often it is necessary to open their eyes, even at the cost of seeming to be incredulous. The testimony of Padre Pio is so interesting that it is difficult to obey the Church when it is recommended that we not express judgment until the Holy Office has issued its own judgments."

Mary Pyle is often compared with Saint Clare. She is viewed as being for Padre Pio what Saint Clare was for Saint Francis of Assisi: an aid in promoting the Franciscan way of life. Some Third Order Franciscans have compared her with Jacopa de'Settesoli, "a holy and noble woman" who, by her charity towards the Franciscans, supported Saint Francis and his followers. Father Bonaventura Massa, O.F.M. Capuchin, Mary Pyle's biographer, compares her with Mary, the sister of Martha in the Gospel, seated in the village of Bethany "at the feet of the Lord and listening to his words" (Luke 19:39).

For my part, I would describe this remarkably generous woman as holy, as filled with charity, goodness, and humility. She never put herself forward, always appearing and speaking simply.

She was a woman from whom one could take so many good examples, especially the example always to live in peace, in tranquility of the spirit. Mary Pyle was a charitable, pious woman who was consistently sweet and good, a person who, for the love of God and in her charity toward everyone, was virtually beyond criticism or suspicion.

Padre Pio the Confessor

ONE morning, Mary told Helena and me about a young woman in northern Italy, named Elena, who, having learned of Padre Pio's Stigmata and of his unusual powers, came to San Giovanni Rotondo to confess to him. Elena, Mary learned, was having an affair with a policeman married to another woman. Elena admitted to Mary that, although she expected to confess her adultery to Padre Pio, she knew that when she returned home, she would continue her illicit affair.

"Imagine how shocked Elena was," Mary continued, "when, after Elena had confessed her sin, Padre Pio refused to give her absolution." Elena went back to confession four more times, and each time, Padre Pio refused to grant her absolution. Finally, before her fifth confession, Elena said to herself: *I would rather die than commit that sin with him again!* With this thought foremost, Elena, in her fifth confession, received absolution from Padre Pio.

There was a man, Mary told us on another occasion, who went to confession every year for five years and only in that fifth year received absolution from Padre Pio. "If you had met him after that confession, however," she said, "you would have seen that his faith was so strong, he could have made converts of stones!"

According to Mary, Padre Pio's life often appeared to revolve around the confessional. She believed he would wish to be remembered primarily as a confessor. "What distinguished Padre Pio from other priests," she said, "was his ability to bring to the mind of the penitent certain sins he or she wished to confess. Padre Pio sometimes mentioned these faults himself, often reminding a penitent of some sin that penitent had neglected to mention in earlier confessions. Padre Pio could tell the penitent just how many times he had missed Mass, the number of promises that had been broken, the mortal sins that had been omitted in the confession, the venial sins that must not be committed again.

"He was paternal. To the extent possible, he was accommodating. Where help and prompting were required, they were given; where bracing and strengthening were required, they too were provided. All sincere men and women were immediately enveloped in the mantle of his sanctity. They came away not only cleansed but keenly aware of what it really meant to sin."

Padre Pio could be both gruff and irate, Mary told us. "He would shut the door in the penitent's face. He could — and did — demolish a penitent's argument with a single, cutting phrase. But at the same time, he immediately recognized insincerity, hypocrisy, or falsehood — and when he did, he lashed out at it, though not from vindictiveness. He loved the human soul too deeply for that. Padre Pio's striking out at one of these human foibles was his way of netting the fish, so to speak. It was his way of recapturing a soul. When he had been rough or angry, the penitent would later be found to have returned to a more chastened disposition, and would be received by Padre Pio accordingly."

Once Mary Pyle told Padre Pio that she had heard it said that without original sin, we would not need redemption. The Incarnation would not have been necessary, and God would not have had a mother.

"That is not true," Padre Pio answered. "God would, too, have had a mother. Christ would not have died on the Cross, but His Incarnation was necessary to bridge the gap between man and

God. Besides, He could not have had a human nature, because it is in man that creation reaches its highest synthesis. Man is the thinking voice of all other creatures. His voice can deny God or make itself an intelligent prayer. Without sin, man would have lived in harmony, and Christ would have been born as the completion of this harmony. (This is true) because it is with Christ, in Christ, and for Christ that everything finds its fulfillment. In this sense, Christ is the alpha and the omega, the beginning and the end. He is the center to which every creature strains. Man is the one who represents every creature. We could say this in a physical sense, too, because our body and our blood are formed of the same material (from which) every other thing is formed. This is true, because, when we die, we return to the earth!''

Brother Leone

EARLY in her residence in her new home, every day Mary could see from her window a shepherd boy who watched his small flock of sheep on the mountainside near her house. In summer, she would rehearse her all-girl choir with the windows open. The shepherd would stand at the window, listen to what was being sung, then learn the song and sing it to his flock.

One day, the boy's singing caught her attention in a particular way, and she invited him into her house. ''What is your name?'' she asked him.

''Leone Mangiacotti.''

''Do you know how to read and write?''

''No. I have never been to school.''

''Do you know the Hail Mary?''

''Yes.''

"Perhaps you would like to become a Capuchin brother someday."

"Would that be possible? But my mother doesn't have the money to send me."

"I will think about that part," Mary told the boy.

And she did. She made it possible for Leone to learn to read and write and later to enter the Capuchin monastery at Salerno. Leone became a courageous Capuchin brother and served for many years among the Capuchin missions in Africa.

The Congregation of the Holy Office

MARY Pyle, who read every book written on the life and work of Padre Pio, felt that the Congregation of the Holy Office (the Church's censor) had denied approval of the ecclesiastical imprimatur to at least fourteen books that reported meritorious work by him. In fact, she said, some books contained false accounts of episodes that reinforced the allegations of Padre Pio's critics. As a collaborator of Doctor Montessori, she recounted the famous educator's remark when she met Padre Pio: "He is a true saint. Without a doubt, his greatest suffering consists of his attempt to hide his condition, at all costs, in order not to infringe on the Church's position."

That was why, she continued, Padre Pio, when he heard talk of miracles and graces, would say tensely: "I count as nothing. Thank God." He was able to tell this to men more easily than women, Mary contiued. Regardless of the social position of penitents who ascended the hill from San Giovanni Rotondo to meet Padre Pio, they were ill prepared to accept humble statements from him. What they really wanted to do was publicly attribute to Padre Pio the gift of omniscience or, if a cure (or perceived cure) were involved, to acknowledge his intervention — all without taking into account the rule of silence demanded by the Holy Office.

Padre Pio's Letters

SOON after settling in San Giovanni Rotondo, Mary was told that Padre Pio had written some profound things in letters to his spiritual children. The letters cover the period from Padre Pio's early youth to the year 1922, when the Supreme Sacred Congregation of the Holy Office forbade him to continue writing. Contained among the writings of Padre Pio — accounts he wrote only out of obedience — are tracts on the Passion of Jesus, the Nativity, the New Year, and the Immaculate Conception, as well as accounts of visions.

Mary asked Padre Pio's spiritual children to borrow his writings, for reading and meditation. Before returning them to their owners, she had them transcribed in order to make them continuously available for contemplation, as food for thought and for her soul. Thus numerous letters are to be found in the archives of the monastery, not only in Padre Pio's handwriting but in Mary Pyle's clear transciption.

In telling Helena and me about Padre Pio's letters, Mary said that some people had been reluctant to let her borrow the letters. Some even told her they wanted to keep the letters private and pass them on to later generations of their families. Numerous people had been willing to share their letters with her, however, she was pleased to add.

Following is a letter transcribed and kept by Mary Pyle. Written to Annita Rodote, a spiritual daughter of Padre Pio's, it concerns the Guardian Angel.

March 2, 1916

Dear Annita,

How consoling is the thought that a spirit stands by each of us. From the cradle to the grave, he does not leave us for an instant, not even when we dare to sin.

This heavenly spirit guides us, protects us as a friend, a brother.

But it is even more consoling to know that this angel prays incessantly for us; he is offering to God all the good acts and words that we perform, and our thoughts and desires if they are pure.

Oh, for the love of charity, do not forget this invisible companion. He is always present, always ready to listen to us, and even ready to console us. A delicious intimacy. Oh, what blessed company this is, if we knew how to understand it!

Keep him always before your mind's eye. Often remind yourself of this angel's presence. Thank him, pray to him, always be good company to him. Be open with him, confide your troubles to him; be continuously fearful of offending his pure gaze. Know him and fix him well in your mind. He is so delicate, so sensitive. Turn to him in the hours of pure anguish. You (will) feel his beneficial effect.

Never say that you are alone in your struggle with your enemies. Never say that you have not a soul to whom to open up and confide. That would be a great injustice to this heavenly messenger.

Padre Pio

Following is another letter. This one written in 1922 to Nina Campile, also a spiritual daughter, on the third week of Padre Pio's "spiritual exercises." It is of particular importance because from it we learn of the tribulations of Padre Pio in his vocation as a member of the Capuchin order and, more important, of the special mission which we believe to have been assigned to him by God: "Sanctify yourself and sanctify others." The means by which this mission was to be accomplished are not spelled out in the letter; rather, they are implied.

San Giovanni Rotondo
November, 1922

May Jesus always be with you. I am on the third week of the holy spiritual exercises, and I am more and more, thanks to the shining grace of God, coming to know myself on one hand and on the other the kindness of Jesus towards me and all others. May this Divine Lover, this cherished spouse of our souls, pray for me, so that I may be able to fulfill the work of grace that he has begun with me a poor soul. In me, poor and worthless creature, who, since my birth, He has deemed worthy of special predilection, He has shown me that He not only will be my Savior, my greatest benefactor, but also the devoted friend, sincere and loyal, the friend of the heart and my treasure of infinite love, of consolation, of joy and comfort. Alas, my heart! Always burning with love for all, while I innocently and unconsciously turned it towards pleasing and welcoming creatures, He always watchful of me, would sweetly and fatherly reproach me, but it was the chastisement that the soul felt. A sad but sweet voice echoes in my heart; it was the voice of the loving Father who outlined in the mind of his son the dangers that he would meet in his life's battle; it was the voice of the Father to the little innocent ones; it was the voice of the loving Father that murmured in the ears and to the heart of the son, to detach himself completely from worldly things (actually from clay and mud) and to jealously consecrate himself entire to Him. Ardently, with loving sighs, with longings that cannot be told with sweet and suave words, He would call him. He wanted him to be all His, moreover, almost jealous of the son loved by him with so much tenderness and affection. He would point out how false and lying was the love that he childishly and innocently gave his creatures. I, the ingrate son, then would understand all and would clearly contemplate the terrible and fearful picture that He, in his infinite mercy, would show me, a picture really that took away all romance, one that would frighten and make the most tested souls tremble. In perceiving the ugliness and miseries of the picture, I would quickly invoke the holy name of Jesus and Mary. In my burning anxiety, I would call upon my good Father, that He might come to my aid. And he, ever ready, at my call, would present Himself to me and, seeing that I was trying to distance myself from the sorry picture, would seem to smile. He would seem to invite me to another life. He would let me understand that the safe harbor, the refuge of peace for me, was in the ranks of the ecclesiastic militia. Where else can I serve you, Oh Lord, but under the flag and in the cloister of the Poor One of Assisi? And He, seeing my embarrassment, would smile. He would smile for long, and this smile would leave in my blood an ineffable sweetness. Sometimes truly I felt Him so near that I almost seemed to see his shadow and my flesh, and all my being exulted in my Savior, in his God. And there I would feel the two forces inside me that would confront each other and that tore my heart in shreds, the world that wanted me for itself and God that was calling me to a new life. (Note: the above refers to the two forces. — Mary Pyle)

My God, who will retell the internal turmoil that went on inside me! Only the remembrance of that intestinal struggle, (which) at that time took place within me, freezes the blood in my veins, and now almost twenty years have passed. . . . The voice of duty told me to obey you, oh true and good God! But my and your enemies would ensnare me, dislocate my bones; they would mock and twist my insides. To obey you, my Lord, this was always the foremost thought in . . . my mind and . . . heart. But I had to assemble so much strength so that I could, with firm and resolute purpose, tramp down the false enticements first, and next, the tyranny of the world that is not yours. You know, Oh Lord, the tears that I spilt before you in these sad times. You know, Oh Lord, of my soul, (of) the wailings of my heart, the tears that ran from my eyes. You had the incontestable proof of those tears and of the cause that I stood for, from the wet pillows where I shed them. I always wanted to obey you, but life also beckoned to me. I wanted to die rather than falter at your call. But you, oh Lord, who, to the end, stood by your son, extended your powerful hand and led me where you had called me. May great praise and thanks be given to my Lord. But you hid me here from the eyes of the world and your great mission, which you had entrusted to your son. This mission was known only to you and me, My Lord! How have I answered this mission? I don't know, but I know that I should have done more, and this is the cause of the restlessness of my heart, this restlessness which keeps on growing within me in these days of spiritual retreat. Rise, then, once again, Oh Lord, and, first of all, free me from myself and do not permit that one, who, with much care and earnestness, you have called and taken away from the world that is not yours, go to perdition. Rise, have entrusted to me, and do not allow anyone to be lost by deserting the (fold) . . . do not permit your inheritance to go to perdition.

  Oh Lord, always make yourself felt in my poor heart, and finish in me the work that you have begun. I intimately hear a voice that constantly says to me: "Sanctify yourself and sanctify others." Well, my dear, this I want; but I do not know how to begin. You must also help me. I know that Jesus loves you, and you deserve it. So speak to Him for me, that he may give me the grace to be a less unworthy son of Saint Francis, that I may serve as an example to my brothers in the organization in such a *manner that my fervor continues as always and that it may grow so as to make me a perfect Capuchin.*

I leave you in the most sacred Heart of Jesus, and I bless you with double affection.

Padre Pio da Pietrelcina

From Mary Pyle's Notebook

MARY was not satisfied. She wished to collect not only what her spiritual father and teacher wrote but also what he said. For that reason she began to write in Italian in a notebook entitled "Words Spoken by Padre Pio." These she wrote down from memory, collected from the pilgrims who came to San Giovanni Rotondo and from Padre Pio's writings on the backs of the prayer cards people gave him to autograph. Here are some examples.

Written in my book, October, 1923, a short time before Padre Pio was forbidden to write:

> *"The good-hearted is always strong; he suffers, but conceals his tears. He is consoled by sacrificing himself for his neighbor (for) God."*

Words spoken by Padre Pio to a young man in the sacristy:

> *"Where there is no obedience, there is no virtue; there is no goodness, no love. And where there is no love, there is no God. Without God, we do not get to Paradise. These virtues form a stairway. If one step is missing, we fall down."*

Words that I heard in the sacristy:

> *"Love and fear should go together. Fear without love becomes cowardice. Love without fear becomes presumption. When there is love without fear, love runs without prudence and without restraint, without taking care where it is going; then other means are needed: punishment."*

The following episode concerns flowers. For Holy Thursday, in the small church of Saint Mary of the Graces, was a beautiful "sepulchre" rich with flowers and brilliant lights. It is usually prepared in this way. But that year, the sepulchre, having been blessed by Padre Pio, had a particular attraction, because it had been blessed by him. After the blessing had been imparted, Mary Pyle devotedly picked up a few of the flowers and preserved them in an envelope in which she wrote: "San Giovanni Rotondo. Flowers that were near the Sepulchre of Holy Thursday 1925, blessed by Padre Pio."

Although at times Mary Pyle's notebook contains accounts of graces received, its central theme is the words of Padre Pio. For example, on one occasion he said to the actor Carlo Campanini: "All come to ask to take away the Cross; no one comes to ask help (in carrying it)." And, on August 28, 1955: "Peace is a reflection of God, and is not had if the soul is not in harmony with God."

In addition to the words of Padre Pio, the notebook contains several stories, or vignettes. Following is one of them, entitled "You Will Never See Your Son's Face Again."

> *In the early years of the Fascist regime, a man living in Bologna became an ardent and violent pro-Fascist. He committed numerous crimes in obeying the dictates of the regime in power. One day, he became most grieved and terrified at seeing his only child stricken by a fatal disease. The man had often heard of Padre Pio and his miraculous powers, so he decided to visit San*

> Giovanni Rotondo to ask Padre Pio to intervene in saving his son's life. He left the child and hastened to San Giovanni Rotondo as quickly as he could, there to plead his case. When the man came before Padre Pio, the latter said: "You will never see your son's face again." And sure enough, when the man returned to Bologna, he learned that the little boy had died and, because the disease that had killed him was contagious, the body had been buried quickly and the gravesite covered with lime.

Another story is entitled "Padre Pio Watches over His Children from Afar":

> A mother of five came with a group of visitors from Bologna to see Padre Pio. She asked him to accept her as one of his spiritual children, and he consented. Because the journey from Bologna to San Giovanni Rotondo was so long and expensive, and because she could not leave her children, five years passed before the woman could once again visit Padre Pio. During that time, not a day passed that she did not, from afar, call upon Padre Pio to "watch over my children," to "protect and bless them."
>
> When she finally managed to return, she went to Padre Pio for confession. After confession she said: "Padre Pio, watch over my children, protect and bless them." To her surprise, he said, somewhat curtly: "How many times are you going to ask me that?" Now thoroughly nonplussed, the woman replied: "But this is the first time I have asked you, Padre," to which Padre Pio replied: "No, you have been saying that to me every day for over five years."

From Mary Pyle's notebook comes a story told to Mary Pyle concerning the cure of a woman's mother in 1921.

> There was a large family in Genoa by the name of Devoto. They were devout people, devoted to Padre Pio. The seriously ill

mother was in danger of losing her leg, if not her life, and a consultation with the doctors had been arranged for the next day.

One of the daughters, alone in her room, was praying that her mother might be healed without requiring surgery. Suddenly the daughter saw Padre Pio standing in the doorway. He was looking at her. The daughter's desire to obtain grace for her mother was so compelling that she did not stop to wonder how Padre Pio could be in Genoa rather than San Giovanni Rotondo, hundreds of kilometers away; nor did she have the slightest doubt that he was actually there in person. She simply threw herself on her knees at his feet and, sobbing and crying, implored him: "Oh, Father, save my mother." Padre Pio looked at her and said: "Wait nine days." The daughter wanted to ask why that particular length of time, but when she raised her eyes, all she saw was an empty doorway. There was no light, no Padre Pio. Once again alone in her room, she returned to her prayers.

The next day, the doctors gave their decision: the only possible way to save the patient's life was to amputate her leg. The daughter, remembering what Padre Pio had instructed her to do, refused to permit the operation. The doctors tried to convince her that she was wrong, that she would be the cause of her mother's early death, that only amputation would save her mother's life. All this was in vain. The daughter was firm in her decision. Even the members of her family, dubious about her insistence on waiting nine days, turned against her — especially when they saw that the mother, instead of getting better, was growing worse day by day. The doctors told her again that, by her stubbornness, she was killing her mother. Though greatly troubled, she could not forget her visitor that night. She would not disobey him; she would wait the nine days, as he had instructed.

When, on the tenth day, the doctors visited and examined the patient, they were astonished to find the leg completely *healed and their patient not only out of danger but on her way to recovery.*

Mother, father, sons, daughters-in-law, grandchildren — all came to thank Padre Pio. But he would not accept their gratitude. Instead, he said gruffly: "Go into the Church, kneel down, and thank Our Lord and the Mother of Divine Grace."

Following is another entry in Mary Pyle's notebook. This one is entitled "Obey Your Father."

Soon after Padre Pio received the Stigmata, the news spread outside the friary, beyond San Giovanni Rotondo. Many read about Padre Pio in newspapers and heard enthusiastic accounts from those who had been to see him. In a city quite distant from San Giovanni Rotondo lived two young girls who wanted to join others who were going to see the priest with the Christ-like wounds, to attend his Mass and receive his blessing. The girls' father, however, did not share their enthusiasm. Because he was a physician, he did not believe the wounds were of supernatural origin, saying that Padre Pio's open, bleeding wounds must be the result of a disease, that he did not wish his daughters to approach the priest and be exposed.

His refusal only increased the girls' desire to go. They pleaded with their father, as daughters know how to when they want something, and eventually he relented somewhat. He would allow them to go to San Giovanni but absolutely forbade them to kiss Padre Pio's hands.

Their joy was so great at having finally received permission and at the thought of seeing Padre Pio that it seemed easy to promise not to kiss Padre Pio's hands.

The longed-for day arrived, and the two sisters, together with other devout visitors, went to San Giovanni Rotondo and with joyful expectation hastened up the road to the friary. Their enthusiasm increased during the Mass. Following the Mass,

Padre Pio went into the sacristy, with all those in the church following. There were many people, and they all passed by Padre Pio one by one, kissing his hands and asking for some special grace, prayer, or blessing. Finally, the sisters, who were well back in the throng, approached him. By now they had entirely forgotten their promise to their father. As they went to kiss Padre Pio's hands, he raised his hands and, in an imperious voice, said, "Obey your father!"

Another entry in Mary Pyle's notebook is entitled "Go, for Holy Obedience." It was told to Mary Pyle by the woman who experienced it.

A good woman from San Giovanni Rotondo, very poor but one of Padre Pio's spiritual children, had come to the friary to confess. Upon leaving the church to return home, she found that it was raining hard. She waited, hoping it would stop; but the time arrived for the church to be closed, and still it rained, now harder than before. The woman told Padre Pio, who had come to the door, that she wished to stay in the church until the rain stopped. That was not possible, he told her. The church had to be closed. "But, Padre," she insisted, "I am not like the rich ladies who have many clothes so that when they get wet, they can change and put on dry clothes. If what I am wearing gets wet, I have no dry clothes to put on and must therefore remain wet. "My child, go, for holy obedience," Padre Pio said. The woman then realized that it was useless to continue insisting. Not possessing an umbrella, she pulled a skirt over her head and shoulders and ran all the way into the town, about two miles away. Although the rain continued to pour down, when she reached her house, she found that she was dry. *It was as though she had not been out in the rain at all!*

In another anecdote from Mary Pyle's writings, a man with a similar experience went to Padre Pio.

He, too, was without an umbrella and was reluctant to go into the town one evening when it was raining hard. He told this to Padre Pio, who encouraged the man to go ahead, telling him to go striaght there, without stopping on the way. The road is entirely in the open, unsheltered by trees, and at that time there were no houses near the road, just a small chapel about halfway between the friary and San Giovanni Rotondo. The man was strongly tempted to stop awhile in the chapel; then he remembered Padre Pio's instruction to go straight to the town, and he obeyed. When he reached the town, he went under a streetlight. He took off his hat and turned it over, expecting rainwater to pour from the brim. To his amazement, he found the hat was dry — not only the hat but his clothes as well; yet it was still raining!

In another anecdote from the notebook, "Why Do You Not Go to Church Every Morning?" a young tertiary used to come often from her home in San Martino to see Padre Pio, her spiritual director. According to the rule:

Members of the Third Order are not supposed to attend dances except with their families in their own homes. But Anna, our young tertiary, loved dancing and frequently went to a friend's house, where she would spend the evening dancing. Before she went to San Giovanni Rotondo, though, Anna always went to confess this fault — not that it was a sin; rather, that it was a fault against the rule of the Third Order. She thereby would not have to mention this fact to Padre Pio.

In Anna's confession one day, Padre Pio asked her whether she attended Mass regularly. "No, Padre, not regularly — not every morning." When he asked why, she explained that to get to

Mary Pyle: Under the Spiritual Guidance of Padre Pio

the church she had to cross the piazza, but that she was shy and thus afraid to cross it. He replied: "but you are not too shy to cross the piazza each evening when you go dancing, are you?" (She took the same route to her friend's houses as she would take to the church.) Anna then saw it was useless trying to hide even small things from her spiritual director; he seemed not only to know practically everything that went on in her hometown, but to possess the ability to look into her heart as well.

Following is another reminiscence from Mary Pyle's notebook, entitled "The Conversion of the Police Marshall."

Anna Trombetta lives in San Martino, where her husband was chief of police. Anna had heard her friends talking about the wondrous friar in San Giovanni Rotondo, and she decided that she, too, would go there and talk to Padre Pio and learn about him and his work.

She returned from her visit to Padre Pio filled with enthusiasm, and told her husband what she had seen and heard about the priest, about, in particular, the perfume, which some noticed when they were near him, while others noticed it when they were at a considerable distance, for example, when calling on him for help or when they were in danger, about the miracles, about Padre Pio's power to look into the hearts and souls of people and there discern little-known facts. Anna was so impressed with what she had heard and seen that she could not sit still. Her husband, though, far from being convinced, ridiculed her, calling her enthusiasm "feminine fanaticism and imagination." He even went so far as to call Padre Pio an imposter.

Undaunted, Anna insisted that, if he was so skeptical, he should go with her to San Giovanni Rotondo; and finally, she persuaded him.

They reached the church in San Giovanni Rotondo and went into the sacristy, along with some other pilgrims. When his turn came to kiss the priest's hand, Padre Pio looked at him and, with tender reproach, said: "Was it not enough that you did not believe in me? What have I done that you should speak against me as you did?" The husband was so overcome when he heard this that, for the first time in many years, he confessed.

Anna and her husband returned to their home in San Martino. For about two months, wherever his police work took him, the husband smelled Padre Pio's perfume. Not only did he smell the perfume, he continually felt Padre Pio's presence at his side. Soon he admitted to Anna that she had not been exaggerating when she told him what a wonderful person Padre Pio was.

From then on, he was as eager as his wife to return to San Giovanni Rotondo. In fact, instead of going to the seashore as they usually did, they decided to spend their holidays near Padre Pio. While at San Giovanni Rotondo, the husband often confessed and took communion. He told Padre Pio that in San Giovanni Rotondo he gladly frequented the sacraments, but that because he was ashamed of his past life at home, he could not summon the courage to do so there. Padre Pio reassured him, saying the time would soon come when he would be mature, when the Lord would give him the necessary strength to attend the sacraments in San Martino.

Her husband became so religious, Anna told Mary Pyle several years later, that she hardly recognized him. He openly frequented the sacraments at home and at Easter took his carabinieri *to confess and take communion. Each night, when he returned home, no matter how tired he was, he would kneel and pray for an hour, saying the Rosary, meditating, and reading spiritual material. He no longer lives in San Martino but has been transferred — more than once. Sometimes (and he is proud of this), he was dismissed from his position because, he was told, the town wanted a policeman, not a seminarian!*

Father Constantino Talks about Mary Pyle

FATHER Constantino, a Capuchin priest who came to visit Mary Pyle one day, remarked to us that when Mary spoke, she did not exaggerate nor exalt herself. When she spoke of Padre Pio, Father Constantino willingly listened to her, not merely because what Mary said moved him but because, even in her admiration for Padre Pio, she managed to strike a balance between admiration and objectivity. If Mary Pyle had included everything she knew concerning Padre Pio in her notebook, Father Constantino continued, she could have filled several notebooks. Following is another anecdote.

> *A girl about twelve years of age arrived from Chicago with her mother. The mother wanted her daughter to receive her first Holy Communion from Padre Pio. The girl and her mother were guests of Mary Pyle in her house, something Padre Pio had requested, the better to prepare the girl for communion. It was understood that, because the girl did not speak Italian and Padre Pio did not speak English, Mary would serve as interpreter, while, of course, keeping the secret of the confessional.*
>
> *At the appointed time, Mary accompanied the girl to the monastery for confession. As they were about to start, Padre Pio turned to the girl and said in Italian, "What is this woman (Mary Pyle) staying here for? Shall we send her away?" When the girl nodded, Mary was asked to leave, and the girl confessed to Padre Pio privately. The confession lasted a considerable time.*
>
> *The curiosity became admiration when the girl later related to Mary Pyle that, in spite of the fact that she did not know one word of Italian, she understood Padre Pio perfectly — what he had said to her and the advice he had given her.*

Raising her hands in amazement as she recounted this miraculous event, Mary Pyle exclaimed: "Oh, what a marvelous thing! What a marvelous thing!"

Life in San Giovanni Rotondo

AFTER accepting Padre Pio's rule over her life, Mary Pyle decided to sell her jewelry and turn over the proceeds to his charities. She wrote to Doctor Montessori, who was holding the jewels for safekeeping, asking her friend to mail them to her. Doctor Montessori thought them too valuable to mail, however, and asked the Capuchin Fathers in Rome to take them. "We don't believe in all this devotion to Padre Pio," they replied, however. "We feel we should not accept the jewels." The fathers were finally persuaded and eventually placed the jewels on a statue of the Madonna that stood in Rome.

Word of Mary's work spread far and wide, and she became known almost as well as Padre Pio. The villagers of San Giovanni Rotondo began calling her "Maria l'Americana" (Mary the American; at Padre Pio's suggestion, Mary had kept her American citizenship). She aided young men in studying for the priesthood, and helped young couples get a financial start in life. When the poor came to see Padre Pio and had no place to stay, she gave them shelter in her house.

During the early years of residence in her house near the monastery, Mary often walked into San Giovanni Rotondo, where she taught catechism to those who requested it, and where she visited the sick, especially those who were alone. At that time there lived in San Giovanni Rotondo a woman named Marianziana. Her face had been nearly destroyed by cancer. About twice a week, Mary visited Marianziana, and when she did, always took something — food, clothes, sometimes medicine. In addition, Mary took something to a child, Donato, who seemed continually to be ill and was in need.

In time, Mary found herself unable to make her regular trips into the village, mainly because, as word of Padre Pio and his work spread, pilgrims were arriving in San Giovanni Rotondo in ever greater numbers, hoping to see him and benefit from his counsel. In these circumstances, Mary, without preference, invited the pilgrims — children, some of them orphans — the destitute — for a meal and, in many cases instruction in the catechism.

Mary rejoiced in seeing numerous guests at her table; "I am content when I see my table full," she was fond of saying. Before long, she had gained the reputation of running a "retreat for great eaters." Even the women in Mary's household, paragons of patience and hard work, said there were so many visitors, especially children who tended to be noisy, that their work was being hindered. Mary defended her hospitality (and her guests), saying in a spirit of Franciscan joy and charity, "They did not ask to come here. *I* invited them!" Not only were they nourished, instructed, and educated, but twelve to fifteen of these children were sent to the Capuchin seminary, all with financial help from Mary Pyle, where they became priests and Capuchin brothers.

Padre Pio's Family

FREQUENTLY Mary Pyle's guests included members of Padre Pio's immediate family — his parents; his older brother, Michael; two younger, married sisters; and Grazia, the youngest member of the family.

By the time of Helena's and my arrival in San Giovanni Rotondo, Padre Pio's two younger sisters, Felicita and Pellegrina, had died, and sister Grazia, a nun, lived in Rome. Padre Pio's brother Michael, lived in San Giovanni Rotondo with Pia, his only married daughter, the wife of Mario Pennelli and mother of eight.

On the Feast of Epiphany that year (the sixth of January), Mary entertained Pia's children at her home with gifts, treats, and games. She asked Helena and me, as teachers, to supervise the games, which we did. There, too, we met Ettore Masone, the son of Padre Pio's sister, Felicita, and Ettore's wife Mariuccia, and their only son, Pio. Pio was baptized by Padre Pio, and Mary Pyle and Mario Pennelli were the godparents.

She profitted by the presence of Padre Pio's parents, Mary said, and would have them tell her about Padre Pio's childhood, which she later included in her notebook. She also wrote (in Italian and in French) a moving account of the death of Padre Pio's mother.

An Episode in the Life of Padre Pio "Told Me by Padre Pio's Mother"

PADRE Pio's mother Giuseppa related the following episode to Mary.

One day, Giuseppa and young Francisco (Francis) were walking along a path. They passed a lovely field of broccoli, and his mother said: "What lovely broccoli! How I would love some!"

"That is a sin," Francisco answered, and his mother had to go without the broccoli.

On another day, mother and son were on their way into the country again, when they saw a lovely tree of figs, and began eating them.

"What?!" his mother cried; "it is a sin to eat broccoli but not to eat figs?"

"Ah," replied Francisco, "the broccoli were recently planted, but the fig tree was planted long ago!"

Following is another episode, also told by Padre Pio's mother, which Francisco often related in later years, much to the amusement of his listeners.

When Francisco was about ten years of age he became ill with an intestinal infection and a high temperature. He was so ill at one point that the physician called in, a Doctor Giacinto, gave Francisco only a few hours to live. Everyone was distraught, and his sisters were weeping. Suddenly, Francisco had an urge to go into the country, and begged his mother to be allowed to do so. At first she resisted, then thought better of it, and Michael put her son on the donkey and took him to "Piano Romana," the family's farm.

It was harvest time, and some farmhands were working in the fields. That day, Giuseppa had fried some peppers, but they were so hot that the men had eaten only a few of them. Thus a large plate was left over and had been put in a chest. Francisco, who loved fried peppers, longed to eat some. He begged his brother to give him one, but Michael, thinking (rightly) that they would not be good for Francisco, gave him only a small amount.

Soon afterward, Francisco, alone with his mother, said, "Close the door; the light bothers me," and, after awhile, "Why don't you leave? I want to be alone awhile." His mother, suspecting nothing of what he was up to, left the room. Once he was alone, Francisco got out of bed and went straight to the chest. He ate all the peppers, then returned to bed. Soon his stomach burned terribly.

When Michael returned, Francisco asked for something to drink. Michael handed him a small bottle of milk, of which Francisco drank about half.

Later, when his mother discovered the empty plate of peppers, she could not imagine who had eaten them. "Has some dog been in here?" she asked. Michael, unaware of what his brother had done, assured her anxiously that he had seen no dog.

Unexpectedly, Francisco's condition improved. Only then did he confess that he had eaten all the fried peppers.

The following episode was told by Padre Pio's father.

When Francisco was older, his father bought him a cap. It was the boy's first real hat. The first opportunity to wear it came on the Feast Day of the "Madonna della Libera," when everyone went to the square to hear music. Francisco happened to be standing in front of a man who was sitting down, and the man could not see because of Francisco's cap. Three or four times, the man asked Francisco to take off his cap, but the boy paid no attention to the request. With his stick, the exasperated man neatly flicked the cap off Francisco's head, and the lovely new cap was thrown on the ground under the feet of some people.

The following episode was told to Mary Pyle by Padre Pio's father.

Zio Grazio — or "Orazio," as most people called Padre Pio's father — said that one day as he watched his elder son, Michael, working in the fields under the hot sun, he turned to the six-year-old Francisco and said: "Francisco, I am not going to let you see the sun." "What do you mean, Father?" asked Francisco.

"I am going to have you study to become a monk," his father answered.

"But, Father," the child said, "that isn't possible. We have no money, and you need money in order to study."

"You need the money. I shall go to America to earn it," Orazio said. This wasn't merely a statement. Orazio was a man of action, a man who did what he said he would do. Although teachers were scarce in Pietrelcina (at the time, there were only two here), Orazio found one, whereupon, true to his word, he left for America to find work.

Mary Pyle: Under the Spiritual Guidance of Padre Pio

The teacher Orazio found was a former priest who had been dismissed from his parish. The teacher, or tutor, could teach Francisco nothing; or rather, Francisco could learn nothing from him. Francisco's mind seemed closed; little or nothing entered it. He even failed to learn to read and write. His interests lay elsewhere. Every morning before class, Francisco would run to the church to serve Holy Mass. His tutor objected to this, maintaining that it was a waste of time, time should be devoted to his studies.

Having given up on the boy, the tutor went to Francisco's mother and told her to send him to work in the fields, to dig and plow. The tutor repeated his assertion that it was a waste of time and money to try to educate the boy; in his opinion, Francisco had no aptitude; his "head was good for nothing." When his mother told Francisco what the tutor had said, the usually mild-mannered boy flared up. "My head is no good?! *His* head is no good — he who is living in sin in his own home!" Where had Francisco, then about seven, learned about the gravity of sin? Who had instilled such a horror of it in him that he closed his mind to all else?

No more schooling, no more lessons. Instead of remaining at home, where he could attend Mass every day, Francisco was taken to the family farm about two miles outside the town. There he sat all day in front of the farmhouse and cried over his changed circumstances. The religious life he had longed for seemed to be vanishing.

Z'Orazio came to this point in the story and suddenly stopped. I looked up in surprise to see tears running down his cheeks. Fifty years had passed since Francisco shed those tears, and still his father could not think of them without weeping.

Francisco's father, far away in the United States, had begun to worry about the tutor in whose care he had left his son. What would the monks say when they heard Francisco had been prepared by such a teacher? Mightn't they refuse to accept Francisco? These and other doubts tormented him. He was working not only materially for his son's future, but to enable him to enter the religious life. He was trying to protect Francisco from the danger of taking the wrong path, and in that teacher he saw precisely that danger. Z'Orazio wasted no time in sending a letter home, telling his wife to find another tutor for Francisco.

One was found, though not without some difficulty. Maestro Caccavo, however, did not wish to accept Francisco in his class. Caccavo owed the other teacher money and was afraid he would offend the man by taking Francisco as a pupil, wishing, above all, to remain on friendly terms. The boy's mother left no stone unturned in her efforts to get Caccavo to change his mind. Failing, she pleaded her case with Caccavo's brother-in-law, who went to the teacher and said: "If you do not accept Francisco Forgione in your school, you will never see your sister in your home again." Thus Francisco was accepted, and the necessary books were obtained. No more tears; instead, study and immediate progress, and in a few months Francisco had covered a year's work. Maestro Caccavo went to Francisco's mother and said: "He is bright. Pretty soon, your son will be teaching *me*."

Francisco continued to make rapid progress. Before long, his teacher proclaimed him ready for examination at the school run by the Capuchin friars and said he would accompany Francisco.

At the friary in Morcone, the Superior took Francisco into a separate room for the examination. Caccavo began to worry. *I should have prepared him. I should have told him how to answer, how to act. He has little contact with anyone other than his parents and me. He will be frightened and won't know how to act.* Caccavo was much relieved when he saw the Superior with his hand on the boy's shoulder. The expression on the Superior's face indicated approval. He said Francisco was well prepared and told them when Francisco was to present himself at the friary.

Their return to Pietrelcina was a joyous one. Like most boys, Francisco wasn't above teasing his mother. He asked Caccavo to let him go ahead, and asked that he not tell his mother what the outcome of the examination had been. Francisco ran ahead, and while I don't know exactly what he said (Padre Pio won't let us tell a small falsehood, even in fun), he let his mother think he had not been accepted. She expressed her disappointment in a torrent of verbal abuse. "I have been wasting your father's money on a donkey! I thought I had an intelligent son, but I have been buying books for a donkey. Go out and dig!"

He let her go on like this for a few minutes then said: "Hurry, Mamma; go and get my clothes ready. I must go to school in a month!"

In school, Francisco was beloved by the Superior and by his fellow students. One day the Superior remarked: "This Francisco Forgione seems to know the rules better than we do — and he observes them better than we do." As an example of the esteem for Francisco, on one occasion, the students were to have a two-day holiday; but some of them objected, saying they wouldn't have enough time to reach their homes before they had to start back. Thinking a request for a longer holiday stood a better chance of being granted if Francisco did the asking, his classmates asked him to go to the Superior. Francisco was shy, however; in addition, he did not like to ask favors of the Superior. At the same time, he hadn't the heart to refuse his friends. His friends persisted, and, summoning all his courage, Francisco overcame his shyness and went to the Superior and asked for an extra day of holiday.

Surprised, the Superior asked why two days wasn't enough, especially since Francisco's home was only a few hours away. Then, before Francisco could proceed with a plausible reason, the Superior hastened on: "Ah, yes; I understand: you are asking on behalf of your friends. Well, there seems to be merit in what you ask. Give them the good news — their holiday has been extended."

Preserving Even the Smallest Things

MARY Pyle preserved with care and devotion the slightest details that in any way whatever had to do with Padre Pio. Once, returning from Rome, where she had been to visit her family who were in Italy for a visit, Mary stopped at Pietrelcina. There, it was decided that she would take Mamma Peppa Forgione to San Giovanni Rotondo for a visit with her son. This was not only a treat for Padre Pio and his mother, but Mary profited from the chance to visit places where her beloved teacher had spent his early years, which, by association, had in her eyes been sanctified.

Mary's care and devotion during the visit is documented by a straw and a flower, now yellowed and withered, that have been preserved. On the envelope in which the two items are kept is written: *Strand of straw from the chair of the house of Padre Pio and a flower from the field where he received the invisible Stigmata.*

In her diary, Mary wrote: "Mamma Giuseppa (Mother Josephine), Padre Pio's mother, arrived in San Giovanni Rotondo December 5, 1928, with me after my brief visit to Pietrelcina. . . . Oh, our fortunate house (on) that December 5th. . . I know now why this house was built . . . Padre Pio (gave) himself completely to the town of San Giovanni Rotondo because God . . . sent him here and . . . entrusted him with (the) souls (of the people in the village). His offering was complete because it included . . . his mother. He made (a) gift of his beloved mother to San Giovanni Rotondo.''

Late one afternoon following benediction services, Mary told us she was sitting with Giuseppa, Padre Pio's mother, and Giuseppa's granddaughter, Pia, Michael's daughter. Since at that time women were permitted in the sacristy, they decided to go there and greet Padre Pio. Shortly after their arrival, Giuseppa suddenly dropped to her knees at her son's feet. Her arms hung limp, and her hands were outstretched. Looking up at her son, she asked him: "How can we know that, in God's sight, we are not great sinners? We try to confess all of our sins. We confess all we remember. But how can we be sure that God does not see many of the sins that we have forgotten or that we do not even recognize as sins?"

At any other time, Padre Pio would not have let her kiss his hand, believing that a son should kiss his mother's hand, not the other way around. This time, however, he permitted her to kiss his hand and to remain at his feet. Looking tenderly into her dark worried eyes, he said: "If we have goodwill and try to confess all our sins, confessing those we remember, God's mercy is so great that it will remove every fault and sin, even those we have forgotten."

In spite of a raging snowstorm on Christmas Eve 1928, Giuseppa insisted that they visit Padre Pio. The next day she was sneezing and had developed a high fever. The doctor said she had pneumonia, and the family gathered at Mary Pyle's to sit with her. When Giuseppa became critically ill, Padre Pio was summoned to administer the last rites of the Church.

Padre Pio, Mary said, came to Giuseppa's bedside to prepare her for the great journey into eternity by giving her the tenderest care. When he presented her with a drink of medicine, those present could see the blood flowing from his wounds to the fingers of his hand. "Padre," the doctor said, "why do you not ask God for the cure of your mother?"

Padre Pio raised his eyes to heaven for a moment, then said sweetly: "God's will be done!"

Giuseppa died four days later. At her death, Mary said, Padre Pio wept profusely. Moved by his tears, the monks asked him why he wept so. "Ah," he replied, "but those are tears of love."

It was a bitterly cold day as the cortege, including the mayors of San Giovanni Rotondo and Pietrelcina, followed the bier to the small village cemetery. There, Orazio and his family said a long, lonely good-bye. Unable to attend because of his physical condition, Padre Pio watched the funeral procession from the front window of the monastery until it was out of sight. For weeks afterward he was heard whispering, "Mother . . . Mother."

Mary Pyle and Padre Pio's Parents

MARY Pyle's love of Padre Pio's parents did not go unnoticed by him. In her notebook, under the heading "Words Said by Padre Pio," she wrote:

Even when Padre Pio was in my house at the time of the death of his mother, an incident occurred. Since I was always near the bedside of dear sick Zia Giuseppa, I did not have a free moment to write to my mother to tell what was happening in the house. I only knew what happened when I sent my mother a telegram giving her the sad news of Aunt Josephine's death. My mother replied, saying: "Padre Pio came again in these days to see me, but I did not know he came to give me this sad news." I asked Padre Pio if it were true that he went to see her, and he replied, "I go continually."

Also included were the words of Padre Pio to some of his spiritual children: "The most beautiful creed is that which bursts from the lips in the darkness, in sacrifice, in pain, in the supreme effort of an inflexible will to do good; it is that which like a thunderbolt rends open the darkness of your soul; it is that which in the flash of the storm lifts you and leads you to God."

Padre Pio also said: "If you suffer with resignation, God is with you, because in resignation to His will you do not offend Him but love Him. And your heart will have great consolation if you think that in the hour of suffering, Jesus Himself suffers in you and with you. He did not abandon you when you fled from Him. Why should He abandon you now that you give Him proof of love in martyrdom?''

"Fear is a worse evil than the evil itself," Padre Pio said on another occasion. "Don't labor over things that generate perturbations and anxieties. One thing only is necessary: to lift the spirit and love God.

Padre Pio was asked on one occasion why there is evil in the world, and he answered: "Listen well. A woman is embroidering. Her son, seated nearby on a low stool, sees her work but in reverse. He sees the knots of the embroidery, the tangled threads, and says: 'Mother, what are you doing? I can't make out what you are doing!' His mother lowers the embroider hoop and shows him part of her work. Each color is in its proper place, and the various threads form a harmonious design. So, we see the reverse side of the embroidery. We are seated on the low stool."

Concerning a question posed to him once about the Blessed Mother, Padre Pio said that when one passes before an image of the Madonna, he or she should say: "I greet you, Oh, Mary. Greet Jesus for me. Beautiful Mother, dear Mother, you are so beautiful. If it weren't for faith, men would make you (into) a goddess. Your eyes shine brighter than the sun. You are beautiful, Mother. I glory in it; I love you. Please! Help me! Let us be grateful to the Madonna, because it was She who gave us Christ."

During his mother's last illness, Padre Pio had come to Mary Pyle's house accompanied by Padre Raffaele. There he remained two days and nights, assisting his mother until her death. Sorrowing over her death, he remained in Mary's house, and, as was their custom, close friends of the family came to offer their sympathy. One who did this was Antoinette Serritelli. At one point, there was a cry from the room adjoining Padre Pio's. "Who is crying so hard?" Padre Pio asked. "Go and see who it is." Antoinette went and returned, saying it was Maria. "Maria? Let her come here."

Mary entered the room but could not speak because of the lump in her throat. "Maria, what is the matter?" Padre Pio asked.

"Nothing," she replied, already becoming calmer.

"Tell me, why are you crying?" Padre Pio asked. "What has happened?"

"I am tormented," Mary said. "I do not know what will happen to this house in the future."

"Even if the house were to collapse," Padre Pio said, "it would be rebuilt stone by stone and put to a use that is good and beautiful."

Mary Pyle never forgot what Padre Pio had told her. In her will she left the house to the Capuchin fathers, to be preserved and passed on to posterity, in memory of Padre Pio of Pietrelcina.

"Go to Mary's House"

NUMEROUS accounts of Mary's charity are documented by the local residents of San Giovanni Rotondo. The following one is by Giovanna Russo.

My younger sister, Maria, and I were young girls at the time. We frequently went to visit Mary, the American, at her house. Once, on the left side of Maria's neck an abscess appeared that was large and deformed.

We used to confess to Padre Pio and afterward sometimes had the opportunity to ask for his advice on practical matters. On this particular occasion, because I was older, I asked him about my sister's condition. "Padre, my sister Maria has an abscess on her neck. We do not know if it is something very serious, and thus our family is worried."

"Go to Mary's house," Padre Pio said. "There is a doctor who is often there — he will provide for your needs."

Indeed, at Mary's house there frequently was a Polish doctor. So we went to Mary's house and told her what Padre Pio had said, and she presented my sister to the doctor. After examining her, he said: "We will make an ointment and apply it." He told us how long the ointment would require to take effect. Then, he said, the abscess would open and secrete pus, and eventually it would disappear.

The doctor soon became interested in my sister's case. In the ensuing days and weeks, he came to our home in the village, accompanied by Petruccio, even in inclement weather, including snow. Many doses of the ointment were applied, and still there was little or no progress. The doctor was in a quandry. He was doubtful about Maria's ability to recover in the present course of treatment. "Why doesn't the abscess break open?" he asked rhetorically. "I am afraid we can wait no longer. We must operate."

Before allowing the operation, however, my sister and I went to Padre Pio. "Padre, the doctor who has been treating the abscess on Maria's neck is urging her to have it lanced. He says he must operate immediately — today."

"Well, let us see if something can be done. Do not fear — nothing bad will happen. No one will operate on the abscess." At that moment, he placed his hand on the infected area on Maria's neck and uttered a prayer.

As we left the church, we met the doctor, who said: "Well, I assume you have spoken to Padre Pio about what I told you. What does he recommend?"

"He says that it is not necessary to operate," I replied quickly. Whereupon we went directly to Mary's house. And shortly after we entered her house, the abscess broke of its own accord, and much fluid was released from it.

The abscess on her neck healed completely, and today she is

alive and well. Perhaps it was the treatment — the ointment — or, perhaps, it was the touch of Padre Pio's hand and his prayer. Whatever it was, no lancing was done, and my sister recovered completely.

House of Mary: First-Aid Post of Charity! Mary Pyle's Compassion and Generosity

AROUND Mary formed a small community of Third Order Franciscans whose lives centered on the monastery: attending Padre Pio's Masses at dawn, a light meal at noon, and religious activities in the afternoon.

Her house began to resemble a branch of the monastery. The Capuchin friars of the province found in Mary Pyle someone ready to help with whatever needed doing. The poor of the village soon came to realize that they had access to a wealthy American who, for love of Padre Pio, had settled on the Gargano Mountain.

Mary Carrabba, a young girl in the church choir, recalled that Mary, the American, as they called Mary Pyle, was generous and big-hearted. Not only did Mary help those who came to her house, and the girls who came for choir rehearsals, but she frequently went into the village and there worked with the sick and old, the needy whatever their age or circumstances. Every time Mary Pyle passed Mary Carrabba's house on a visit of charity or to instruct the children in catechism, she would stop in front of the balcony of their house and call out: "Maria! Philomena!" And Mary Carrabba and her sister would run out to greet her. Their meetings were always warm and cordial.

Not far from their home, in a part of the village at a higher elevation, lived Marianziana Emerenziana, a poor woman ill with cancer which had already disfigured her face. Mary Pyle visited

Marianziana and helped her with gifts and words of comfort. All who saw Mary on their street knew she was on her way to visit Marianziana, but, Maria said, they had gone once with Mary Pyle and had become so depressed at the condition of the ailing woman that they did not want to go there anymore. Instead, every Friday, "Maria the American" went into the village to teach the children their catechism, and on her way, would stop by to visit Marianziana.

According to Josephine Palumbo, another girl who had been in Mary's choir, it was Mary who prepared Josephine for her first Holy Communion. Mary even gave Josephine her white dress for the ceremony. In addition, Mary prepared the young girls for various recitations presented in the small theater of the Missionary Room to benefit the Capuchin missions in foreign countries. Occasionally among the spectators, sitting in the front row, would be Padre Pio, who called Josephine "Little Gypsy," in reference to her part in the performance. When she went to kiss his hand afterward, Padre Pio would say "Brava." At Mary Pyle's death, as she watched the cortège pass, Josephine was reminded of the deeds of this wonderful woman. She felt that a saint had left this world.

Felicita Massa, a woman in the village, told us that she went to Mary Pyle's house one day to ask for a donation for the seminary, only to learn that Mary was ill and in bed. Having been told by a member of her household that Felicita was there, Mary sent word that Felicita was to come upstairs to Mary's room. After asking Felicita to sit down, Mary expressed her pleasure at seeing her after such a long time. "You came at the right time," Mary said. "I just finished a beautiful meditation." Felicita recalled that the last time they had seen each other must have been the last Sunday after Pentecost. "I have discovered in the epistle of the Mass today the secret of happiness!" Felicita did not remember where the exact quotation was found, but it was the letter in which Saint Paul says: "You Christians, stay away from slander, unchastity, wickedness, and greed which is idolatry." St. Paul continued, I recommend that you love the opposite of that paganism — a Christian life — an inventory of virtue which is the practice of goodness, charity, chastity and generosity. And, Mary Pyle said, "Behold, it is enough to live according to this teaching of Saint Paul, because I can be saved *and* be happy!"

A local woman named Graziella, married to a farmer and the mother of nine, said that Mary Pyle was a good Christian who helped everyone and who did much charitable work. Once, Graziella recalled, she was in debt to someone and could not repay the loan. She went to Mary and asked her to "loan me the equivalent of about fifty dollars."

"As soon as we make the harvest," she told Mary, "I will return the money to you." And Mary, apparently without giving the matter a second thought, gave Graziella the money.

Graziella, of course, hoped to have some money left after the harvest with which to repay the loan. Alas, this did not happen. Graziella went to Mary and, crying, told her there was no money left from the harvest. "What shall I do?" she asked, but Mary merely raised her hand. When Graziella asked what the gesture meant, Mary replied, "It means that I remit the debt and that you owe me nothing."

Brother Gerardo Natale

FOR many years Brother Gerardo Natale had prepared the hosts for Masses celebrated in the monastery church of San Giovanni Rotondo, and during that time the number to be prepared had steadily increased. In addition, Brother Gerardo met the visitors who came with requests that he convey their petitions to Padre Pio. With the latter responsibilities, Brother Gerardo could not make the hosts during the day, and instead made them at night, which left only a few hours' rest in each twenty-four-hour period. As a result, he was always fatigued — a situation that the Father Superior noticed. He suggested that Brother Gerardo ask Mary Pyle if she could take over the work and, if so, could she do it in her house. Agreeing that this was an excellent idea, Brother Gerardo went to see Mary, who gladly accepted, adding with a smile: "I can aspire to no greater honor than to work for Jesus in the Blessed Sacrament. I will begin immediately!"

So, from that day until her death, Mary prepared the hosts for the Eucharist — attending to every detail, checking each host individually to make sure no loose particles were on it. Later, when the Capuchin fathers opened a mission in Eritrea, Mary helped by organizing a small workshop for the mission in her house, where Nina Noveilli, of Cerignola, directed the cutting, sewing, and crocheting and about a dozen girls made vestments and other articles for the altars. Occasionally vestments were sold to raise money for the mission; in addition, Mary contributed generously whenever the Capuchin missionaries visited San Giovanni Rotondo.

Life in Mary's House

BETWEEN the monastery and Mary's house there was a continuous coming and going of friars, the group that gathered around Mary, and others. Mary was visited by children whom she had encouraged and helped in their studies; by numerous Capuchins from throughout the province; by seminarians from Pietrelcina, Vico Garganico, and Sant'Elia a Pianisi. Everyone — not just the seminarians but philosophy and theology students too — considered Mary a second mother. Visitors to San Giovanni Rotondo would recall an anniversary, some event or occasion in Mary's life, which would immediately be converted into a cause for sacred and innocent celebration in the form of wholesome music and song. Among these friends, these consecrated Franciscans, Mary felt at ease and would join them.

Mary apparently could no longer conceive of a life other than her present one, that among the Third Order Franciscans. She had virtually no private life; for she was available to any and all whenever they happened to call on her. When friends called on her, they typically found her seated at the head of a long, dark wood table, usually with a pile of letters before her. Nearby, or in adjoining rooms, were various people from the community, intent on such tasks as ironing, cooking, and reading. To complete the scene, a humble woman from the village sat in a corner, awaiting mealtime.

At Mary Pyle's table seating was without preference for rich or poor. The poorest diner sat elbow to elbow with, say, an intellectual; local dialects intermingled with the elegant university talk of Oxford, Berlin, Paris. Sitting at the head of the table would be Mary — serene, frequently smiling, switching from Italian to English to French to German so easily that hardly anyone noticed the change.

Few realized how large a group Mary had in the house. Without warning, a knock at the door would announce the arrival of a friend, a stranger, or a beggar. For the forty-five years that she lived in San Giovanni Rotondo, this was Mary Pyle's way of life.

In conversation, Carmela, the manager of the household, talked about Mary Pyle's life in considerable detail. We asked Carmela if she could confirm that Mary sometimes came out of Padre Pio's confessional with tears in her eyes. Yes, she said, this sometimes happened, but for what reason she did not know. She thought it possible that when Mary asked for favors for members of her family, Padre Pio had suggested to her that, to obtain grace, she participate in suffering.

Mary lived an austere life. Throughout the time Carmela

knew her, Mary wore the brown habit of the Capuchins, but without the cowl. (When she went to the United States, though, she wore a brown overcoat over the habit.) It was Mary's custom to sleep on a hard bed (with a mattress of wool) that more closely resembled a table. One night when Padre Pio's mother was gravely ill, Mary told Carmela, Padre Pio slept in Mary's bed and Father Raffaele, the Father Superior of the monastery, slept in a bed near him. The next morning, Padre Pio said to Mary: "Mary daughter, how can you sleep on a bed that is so hard?"

Mary allowed herself few amenities. During her early years in San Giovanni Rotondo, she would listen to the news on her radio; but the young people who came for choir rehearsals wanted to listen to modern, popular music on it, so Mary removed the radio and gave it away. She never had a television set in her house. When Carmela came to her in 1937, she had a telephone, but the neighbors soon took advantage of its availability. Later, when electricity had to be conserved and there were frequent problems with bad weather, the telephone was removed. It wasn't until Mary became ill years later that the phone was reinstalled for use in emergencies.

Mary Pyle, of course, always ate moderately, scrupulously following the rules on fast days, just as the monks did. On Good Friday, and for the important feasts of the Madonna and Saint Francis, she would eat only one vegetable, and this on her knees, after having recited the "Miserere" (Lord, have mercy). Mary followed this form of penance for many years, until her health would no longer permit kneeling on bare floors.

Mary continued the Eucharistic tradition of fasting, beginning at midnight, although the Vatican II Council had given permission to partake of food and drink until an hour before receiving Communion. Late in her life, in order to attend Padre Pio's early Mass, she took a few drops of medicine prescribed in the treatment of a heart condition. Also, reportedly she followed as closely as possible the monk's practice of rising at midnight for prayers and reciting the Divine Office. According to Carmela, Mary always recited the

Divine Office in Latin, following the Roman Breviary used by the Capuchin Fathers. She would not go to bed until she had finished the prayers mandated for the office that day.

A Typical Day

A TYPICAL day for Mary began with her rising around 4:00 in the morning and, just before 5:00, going with members of her household to Padre Pio's Mass. Following Mass and Holy Communion, she remained in church for extended thanksgiving and meditation. Then, if a religious function was scheduled that day which required music, Mary went immediately to the organ and took her place.

She would return home at various hours and have breakfast, after which she turned her attention to other work. If, however, on arriving home, she found people waiting who had come from other towns or even from other countries, Mary, who spoke several languages, would listen and then tell her visitor or visitors what the situation was and how they should approach Padre Pio (for that was often the reason they had come).

When special religious functions were scheduled at the church, Mary conducted the choir rehearsals and played the organ. Then, too, there seemed to be an unending stream of correspondence that had to be attended to; for letters from around the world arrived daily, generally concerning Padre Pio and his work. In addition, the hosts for Communion had to be made, which Mary and the members of her household did in Mary's house. It was work that they enjoyed. Finally, rounding out the day's activities, Mary and her co-workers prayed together.

After the ritual blessing at dinner (served at noon), a spiritual reading was conducted that was similar to the monks' readings at the monastery. In subsequent years, primarily because strangers often were present, the readings occasionally were omitted and eventually were eliminated altogether.

Immediately after the first course of the meal, Mary and the members of her household would, according to custom and with everyone holding their arms outstretched, recite five Our Fathers and five Hail Marys and a Glory be to the Father.

In the early years of Mary's residence in San Giovanni Rotondo, Mary would, at about three in the afternoon, go to the seventeenth-century church of the Capuchins and there recite the Divine Office with the friars. Often accompanied by one or more members of her household, she would be on the first floor in front of the tabernacle, and the friars were upstairs with the choir.

As the fame of Padre Pio spread, a 4:00 p.m. vesper service was instituted for the public. The rosary was recited, the litany was sung, the Blessed Sacrament was recited, and Padre Pio gave the benediction. Mary played the hymns at the portable organ and the choirgirls of the Scola Cantorum sang.

Every Thursday, Mary awoke at midnight for an hour meditation on Jesus' Agony in the Garden. Any member of her household was free to participate. Sometimes the meditation was held on the first floor and sometimes in Mary's bedroom.

Enrico Zeni

AMONG the members of Mary's household was Enrico Zeni, a handyman who ran errands and served as general repairman. In 1936 he and his brother, Ernest, had come from northern Italy to visit Padre Pio and had become fascinated with the Stigmatist, so much so that they determined to find work and remain near him. Both men worked awhile for Mary; but after two years, Ernest went elsewhere to find work. At the time my sister and I were introduced to the brothers, they had become chimney sweeps, and, indeed, their skins *were* black. "The chimney sweep brothers may have black skins because of their work," Padre Pio commented, "but their souls are as white as snow!"

Enrico — who remained with Mary for thirty-two years, continuing at her house for six months after her death — discussed his memories of Mary Pyle with Helena and me. For instance, Mary used to walk the two miles to and from the monastery to the village of San Giovanni Rotondo, where she instructed children in catechism. (This we had heard from others, but it was interesting to have it corroborated.) She was consistently generous with the Capuchins, helping the secular priests as well, and made contributions to the poor in the form of money, clothing, and household items. She helped the Capuchin brothers financially, which made it possible for several of them to become priests of the order.

The Mission Workshop

MARY Pyle was in many ways an extraordinary woman — possessed of great kindness and charity, of love for her neighbor without measure or distinction. Because she possessed these qualities in abundance, Mary was capable of tolerating most of life's vicissitudes. For example, she disapproved of criticism and gossip about anyone, whether it concerned monks, priests, or laypeople. She sought tranquility even when faced with conflict among those in her household.

It was Mary's custom after returning home from services, about twilight, to recite the Divine Office then spend the evening at her writing. On numerous occasions, usually when she was to confess to Padre Pio the next morning, she wrote until the early hours of the morning. After confession, she would turn over to

Padre Pio the contributions she had received the day before. The contributions were divided into three groups — that for the Casa Sollievo hospital, that for Pietrelcina, and that for the monastery — according to the intent of the benefactor.

Another project of Mary's was the organization of a missionary workshop in her home, to benefit the foreign missions of the Capuchins. In the workshop young women made vestments, priestly garments, and other types of clothing, usually of linen; and these were sent either directly to the foreign missions or sold and the money turned over to the missions.

As Padre Pio's fame spread, the name Mary Pyle was mentioned more and more in publications about Padre Pio. When he was discussed in the media, it was safe to assume that Mary would be mentioned, too.

She was renowned among the people of San Giovanni Rotondo, both for her charity and for her kindness toward people, which seemed to know no bounds. Every day, people of social rank as well as ordinary men and women came to Mary's house. To maintain some semblance of order, however, and to monitor and control to the extent possible those who appeared at her door asking for charity, it was suggested that she limit the dispensing of charity to one day per week. Reluctantly consenting, Mary chose Friday.

Sometime after this policy went into effect, a poor woman appeared, asking for help. The member of Mary's household who met the woman at the door told her that, since it wasn't Friday, little could be done for her that day. To this, the woman replied: "Yes, I know today is not Friday. But Friday is the only day I eat!" Mary, hearing the exchange between the two women, came to the door and inquired what the matter was. When told, she said: "You did well, You were right to come!" Whereupon the woman was given some food.

Padre Pio and Rome

THE controversy involving Padre Pio began in Rome. Pope Benedict XV — who held the office from 1914 to 1922 and was pope when, on September 20, 1918, Padre Pio, a Capuchin friar, became the first priest in the history of the Church to receive the stigmata — looked upon Padre Pio with a certain benevolence. "Padre Pio," he said to Monsignor Damini one day, "is one of those whom God from time to time sends to convert mankind. (We should) take on the task of making him better known. He is not appreciated (as much) as he deserves."

In 1922, Cardinal Ratti was elected pope and became Pius XI. It was during his pontificate (1922-39) that the controversy, investigation, and finally the persecution of Padre Pio began. Whereas Benedict XV had viewed him with approval, Pius XI condemned the friar of the Gargano, condemnation mitigated only slightly by the counsel of Cardinal Gaspari, the Vatican's secretary of state and the father of the series of concordates issued during the 1930s.

The trials and tribulations of her beloved Padre Pio became Mary Pyle's as well, something she demonstrated many times over during her long life. Throughout the two years of Padre Pio's confinement she prayed diligently that the restrictions be lifted. From June 11, 1931 to July 15, 1933, Padre Pio remained segregated in the monastery, forced to celebrate Holy Mass in the interior chapel (he was not allowed to descend into the church). One can imagine the sorrow and distress of his disciples during that time.

Journalists who came to interview Mary, among them reporters from *Time* and *Life*, asked about Mary and her work; but what they were really interested in was Padre Pio and his work and the controversy surrounding him. And Mary responded to their questions. The interviews, though, led some in the village of San Giovanni Rotondo to believe she was contributing to the difficulties that had befallen Padre Pio starting on June 11, 1931. When the Vatican placed restrictions on him during the investigation of his stigmata and his remarkable (to some, miraculous) work. With the exception of the Mass — which was to be celebrated privately in the inner chapel of the monastery, with only one server present — he was suspended from every ministry. When Padre Pio learned the extent of the restrictions placed on him, he said: "The will of God must be done."

His daily routine during this segregation included celebration of the Mass (about two hours); prayer in the choir (until noon); an hour of study in the library; and, in the afternoon, more prayers, from vespers until midnight. He was permitted no contact with anyone outside the monastery.

Meanwhile, the villagers, maintaining that Mary had given information to journalists who took and sensationalized it, ostracized her. No one other than members of her household spoke to her. For weeks on end, Mary could not take a walk without encountering the villagers with their stony, accusing stares. She suffered terribly, Mary said in later years, not only from the rejection but from being denied confession to Padre Pio. Even when she attended daily Mass and received Holy Communion, villagers taking communion would move away from the altar rail, leaving her alone to receive.

Eventually an investigation resulted. The monks, realizing that the investigation of Padre Pio went much deeper than the accounts Mary had given to journalists would indicate, frequently chased the women away; but Mary had too much sorrow in her heart to appreciate the monk's sympathy for her and for Padre Pio. Even when her angora cat had a litter of kittens, and she wanted very much to share the news, no one in the church would listen.

Confinement and Release of Padre Pio

ONCE, during the first year of the restrictions on Padre Pio, Mary walked the fifteen miles to and from Saint Michael's shrine in Monte Santangelo; a year later she again walked to the shrine but this time remained in the village overnight. During the time when Padre Pio's case was being investigated in Rome and he was permitted no contact with people, the Capuchin fathers at his monastery recommended that people not talk about him, that everyone maintain a discreet silence on the matter, hoping thereby to create a better climate of opinion, one that would work to counteract those in positions of power who were arrayed against Padre Pio. In the view of the Capuchin fathers, silence — or, at least, restraint — was the appropriate behavior for all concerned, including Mary Pyle. Although Mary followed their recommendation, one day she asked: "How can I be silent about Padre Pio? I feel ready to burst! I want to shout, to tell everyone who this man really is!"

Finally, in 1933, Pope Pius XI revoked the decrees, commenting as he did so: "Now you Capuchins will be glad. It is the first time in the Church's history that the Holy See (has retracted) its decrees. It isn't that I am against Padre Pio; it is only that I was misinformed about him." Then, July 16, 1933, Padre Pio celebrated Holy Mass in the church. Among the faithful attending the service was his devoted and solicitous disciple, who, from the first day of Padre Pio's segregation, had prayed for this happy day to come.

Before she went to church, though, Mary picked a daisy from her garden, intending to offer it to Padre Pio as a memento of his release from the investigation and persecution. At the end of the Mass, Mary waited impatiently for a chance to greet Padre Pio, her spiritual father and teacher. When he finally stood before her, she offered him the daisy she had picked, as a symbol of her faith and love. Moved, Padre Pio accepted the flower, kissed it and pressed it to his heart. Then, after a moment and without a word, he handed it back. Mary, ever the disciple, preserved the flower, wrapping it in paper on which she wrote: *The day that Padre Pio descended for the first time to celebrate Mass in Church, on July 16, 1933, (he) has kissed this flower and pressed it to his heart.*

A few weeks later, Mary joined some other women from the village waiting to confess to Padre Pio. In the confessional she had barely knelt when he said loud enough for all the women outside to hear: *sciagurata!* (wretched one!) Three times he repeated the word. Humiliated, Mary looked at the women as she came out of the confessional. Many of them were smiling. When she asked Padre Pio on a later occasion why he had said "that ugly word to me in my last confession," he replied: "My dear daughter, had I not said that word to you, some of those women would have killed you, (because of) the terrible resentment of you that they had in their hearts." Mary now understood the gravity of what Padre Pio was saying to her. She was relieved to learn that the reason wasn't that she had committed some sin against God.

Gradually, in time, the stony silence of the villagers gave way, and Mary once again was accepted.

Wartime

WITH the coming of World War II, the Italian authorities ordered Mary, an American citizen, interned in Pietrelcina; there she remained from December 1941 to October 1943. Years after these events, Father Emilio of Matrice told us how Pietrelcina came to be chosen.

In Rome to give a lecture, Father Emilio received word from his Father Superior to meet Mary Pyle at the office of the minister of foreign affairs. When they arrived, they were asked to sit down, Mary as the interested party and Father Emilio as her guarantor, or "relative." Mary was told that she must register as an alien. With a look as though he were annoyed, the minister asked numerous questions — some worthwhile, some not. Finally he came to what apparently was the object of their meeting; permission to make a search. At that, Mary became alarmed. Her face reddened and her eyes filled with tears. She did not respond to the minister's request. On the contrary, she appeared to have fainted. Thinking she needed air, the minister and Father Emilio hurried to help her. They unbuttoned her coat, only to discover that Mary wore the clothing of a Capuchin: habit, cord, rosary, and, around her neck, a chain with a crucifix. The minister seemed unable to find his voice. Raising his hand, he stammered: "She looks like the Sorrowful Madonna!" — and he promptly turned around and sat down. After a few minutes he resumed speaking. "This is not a simple person. She is a truly religious woman."

They conversed amicably for awhile, then the minister asked Mary for prayers. "No, no minister," she said; "I am not a saint. The saint is our Padre Pio!" And the minister rescinded his earlier request for permission to make a search.

Mary was sad to be leaving San Giovanni Rotondo. She wondered where they would send her, if not to a camp for political prisoners and other "undesirables." At that point in the discussion, Father Emilio proposed to the minister that Mary be confined as a political prisoner in Pietrelcina, Padre Pio's paternal home. The minister agreed, and permission was granted. Mary, happy to go to Pietrelcina to stay in the house where the spiritual father of her heart had once lived, was so glad at the decision that she wanted to kiss the minister's hand.

The Forgione Home

THE house where for two years Mary Pyle was a "political prisoner" is located in the "Castle District," which takes its name from a medieval castle around which a group of structures were built. The small houses of the village are packed close together. The streets are so narrow that they cannot be entered by automobile. Long ago, the steep ascents required the cutting of steps in the rock; so there is no roadway. An automobile is left at some distance, and one walks uphill to one's objective along the same paths and alleyways that Padre Pio took in his youth. His old home is preserved in virtually its original condition: the rough stone floor; the unadorned walls; an open fireplace of cooking; the small bedroom where Francisco was born; the "tower room" across the narrow street, named for Our Lady of the Angels, where, as a student, Padre Pio went during the day to pray and study. The house's furnishings — the kitchen utensils and simple equipment which served the family's needs — are still there.

From any window of the house in which Padre Pio was raised, the view is spectacular: a wide, rolling valley with well-cultivated fields stretching away to the mountains of the Sannio region, an offshoot of the Apennine chain. In Italy, the visitor invariably is met with cordiality and smiling faces, with generous hospitality and respect. With impressive simplicity, the local people invite their visitors to join them for a family meal, where the fare is plain but offered with grace and dignity.

Life In Pietrelcina

IN the sixteenth century, Pietrelcina (literally, "little rock") had about a thousand inhabitants. Since then, the population has risen and fallen, depending on circumstance — war, pestilence, or some other scourge. In the last hundred years or so, emigration to the United States has been the dominant cause of population decline, though in the 1980's the population stabilized at about 3,000. In addition to the charm it retains from earlier times, Pietrelcina is enriched by the fact of its illustrious son, the Capuchin, Padre Pio.

During Mary's stay in Pietrelcina, she was not permitted to go into anyone's home other than that of Padre Pio's family. She was, however, allowed to take walks of three kilometers each day with Catherine Florio, a woman from the village. Mary was happy for this chance to get out. "I felt as though I had been released from prison," she said once. And, indeed, that is pretty much what it was; for much of the time between 1941 and 1943, Mary was under what amounted to house arrest, although, later, when the police marshal got to know Mary — to know her goodness, her charity, her self-confidence — he permitted her to go into the homes of the villagers.

Mary did not abandon her spiritual life just because of the war and her forced stay in Pietrelcina. She attended Mass daily and took Communion, followed by the divine office and vespers.

One might ask: To what extent did the inhabitants of Pietrelcina accept Mary Pyle? Following are two examples. According to Catherine Florio, Mary's conversation was always filled with wisdom. She was such an interesting conversationalist that, once you had conversed with Mary, you were not likely to forget her.

The other example was that of Padre Pio's physician, Doctor Cardone. Considered the village's intellectual when he was young, the physician would often stop and converse with Mary. He and numerous others in the town were fascinated with her. Of Mary's sojourn in Pietrelcina, he said: "This woman Mary Pyle is truly exceptional. I have never known a woman so kind, so good, so detached from the grandeur of the world that (the rest) of us are (so) attached to!"

Pia Pannullo lived near the home of Michael Forgione, Padre Pio's brother. Pia's husband was a prisoner of war, and she lived in Pietrelcina with her child. In conversation with Mary Pyle one day, Pia told Mary that she could not go to Mass on Sundays or Holy Days because she had no one to watch her young child. Mary immediately volunteered to attend the first Mass, then return to watch the child while Pia went to the second Mass. Pia gratefully accepted Mary's offer; and so, for the love of God, Mary Pyle briefly became a babysitter!

Throughout the time she was in Pietrelcina, Mary attended Mass daily. To reach the church in time for early morning services, though, she had to cross a field in the dark that was filled with potholes. One morning as she was returning from Mass, a young German soldier came out of the woods adjoining the field; at gunpoint, he ordered her to stop, asking her where she had come from and where she was headed. Much to the soldier's surprise, Mary answered in fluent German. He was so pleased that he went with her to the Forgione home, where he was given food and drink. Mary became concerned, however, when she noticed that the soldier was overly attentive to the attractive, dark-haired Pia Forgione. Worried that he would molest the girl, Mary prayed silently to Padre Pio; and her prayers were answered, for eventually the soldier left quietly.

Father Ezechia

FATHER Ezechia Cordone, a Franciscan priest in Pietrelcina, told us about his first encounter with Mary Pyle. It was during the summer of 1943, toward the end of Mary's stay in Pietrelcina. There, Father Ezechia would meet Mary in church, at the Sisters of the Most Precious Blood, or at some other religious function. He even served as her confessor. When he met Mary, Father Ezechia said, she had the reputation of a person of superior culture and intense spirituality — a reputation confirmed as he came to know her. Father Ezechia saw in Mary Pyle a person of great faith, profound humility, luminous smile, and great serenity. Each time he encountered her, he found Mary serene and smiling, even when her health indicated otherwise or when the sorrows and persecution visited upon Padre Pio caused her emotional suffering. Never did Mary say anything against the measure imposed on Padre Pio, or against those she believed responsible for Padre Pio's problems. Though outgoing in her relations with people, Mary assiduously avoided the careless, corrupting word that could hurt and wound.

Each encounter reinforced Father Ezechia's impression of a serenity and spiritual calm about Mary Pyle. To him, her purity of heart, submission to obedience, love for the poor, and diligent prayers were testimony of such power that he determined to live a better life and to reconsecrate his life to God.

Return to San Giovanni Rotondo

ON the night of October 4, 1943, American troops reached Pietrelcina. That night, Mary ran as far as the bridge outside the village, where she embraced as many of the soldiers as she could, as a mother embraces a son who has been away for a long time. The arrival of the Allies meant that she and many others were now free to return to San Giovanni Rotondo. Although the war raged on in northern Italy and throughout much of Europe, for Mary, liberation was now a reality.

Two days later, Mary was in a wagon belonging to a villager, David Aucone, on the road to San Giovanni Rotondo. According to David, who drove the wagon, the trip was a near disaster. The large farm wagon had to contend with a great deal of refugee traffic; it seemed that all of Italy was in transit, either fleeing the retreating Germans or rushing to embrace the advancing Americans and British. Also, the roads had been heavily damaged in the fighting, and nearly all the bridges had been destroyed. Mary and David had to ford a river, and there were sudden thunderstorms, with heavy rain and frequent periods of walking. For these and other reasons, what should have been a day's journey by automobile took three days.

Prayer was Mary's mainstay during the journey. Throughout, she was consistently cheerful, always content. She never appeared to be agitated, never lost patience. On the contrary, Mary seemed to thrive on adversity. Sustained by a mysterious inner strength, she drew on that strength each time some new misfortune befell them.

Whenever Mary and David arrived in a town, usually having been without food and water since the previous evening, the first thing Mary did was seek out a church and a priest to give her Holy Communion. At one point in the journey, as they reached the town of San Marco of Cavoti, it was raining and they were soaked to the skin. Nevertheless, Mary found the local church and took Communion. With that done, all traces of fatigue seemed to leave her.

Hospitality to Soldiers

IN conversation one day we told Mary that we had a brother named Carmen who was killed in World War II and was buried in Florence, Italy.

Then Mary told us that her house was always open to soldiers during World War II — Allied, German and Italians alike. She said that she turned no one away, instead inviting them to stay for a meal in her house. Even when the meal had been prepared only for her and the members of her household, it seemed that Divine Providence provided and that there was always enough for everyone.

Every Sunday, soldiers came up from their camp near Foggia, in groups of as many as fifty; and Mary said she would tell them about Padre Pio. Two of the soldiers who came to her house regularly, Daniel and Clement, later became Capuchin priests. Some of the soldiers told her that they believed their survival in combat had been due to Padre Pio's blessing.

American women also served in the military, and some who were stationed nearby came to Mary's house. One in particular, an American Indian, had the special assignment of assisting paratroopers. Mary Pyle helped arrange a meeting between the soldier and Padre Pio. Because the face of the girl (she *was* young, as were so many soldiers) seemed to express an untranslatable kindness, Padre Pio said to her when they met: "Your eyes tell the goodness of your soul." Her mother was Catholic, but her father had converted to Catholicism only four years before his death. When the girl told Padre Pio of her father's death, he said: "Your father has stolen Paradise!" Thereafter, the girl often came to visit Padre Pio and Mary Pyle.

My sister and I had heard rumors of unsuccessful attempts by the Americans to bomb San Giovanni Rotondo. One day I asked

Mary about the rumors. "Oh, yes," she replied; "a group of citizens afraid of bombing raids approached Padre Pio, who assured them that "not a bomb shall fall on . . . San Giovanni Rotondo." Then she told us the following story.

In July 1943, the city of Foggio and the surrounding area were at the center of an area designated for bombing. It was the twenty-sixth of the month, the feast of Saint Anne. In the sky over San Giovanni Rotondo there appeared a squadron of bombers. Later, it was learned that the town's large school building had, falsely and treacherously, been reported to be a storage depot for munitions. The bombing raid was unsuccessful. Later, in talking to Mary Pyle, the airmen said they had seen a peculiar white cloud in the sky and in the cloud three persons — a monk with a beard, a woman holding a child in her arms, and a young man carrying a sword that dripped with blood. The bombers made two passes over the town but were unable to release their bombs apparently because of a jammed release switch.

At the war's end, numerous American soldiers, from Foggia and from Amendola (about fourteen miles farther away), came to see Padre Pio and Mary before leaving for the front (or, for some, home.) Among the soldiers were the airmen who had taken part in the attempted bombing of San Giovanni Rotondo. Mary accompanied them to the monastery and presented them as a group to Padre Pio. When they saw him, some of them said: "Look, it's the monk we saw in the cloud on that raid. His hand was covered with a fingerless glove." And, Mary said, when she took them into the church and they were standing before the Madonna of the Graces, they said: "This is the woman holding the child in her arms that we saw."

Shortly thereafter, Mary went with the soldiers to the grotto of Saint Michael at Montesantangelo, a few miles outside San Giovanni Rotondo. When they saw the beautiful statue of Saint Michael the Archangel, they exclaimed: "Oh, this is the young man we saw in the cloud, his sword dripping with blood!"

Mary could only conclude that Padre Pio had kept his promise not to let a bomb fall on San Giovanni Rotondo. In time, I heard Mary relate this account to numerous others who came to visit her.

Young and lively, the American soldiers seemed to take over the village. As young and brash as they might be, however, they invariably let themselves be subdued by Padre Pio with a clasp of the hands. Many of them went to him for confession. One might wonder how they confessed, when few spoke Italian, and Padre Pio spoke no English. Yet when Mary would ask them upon their return from confession, "How did you confess? Padre Pio does not speak English," they would answer: "That's his affair. He told us what we need to know!" Then she would serve them snacks or, if they came at noon, dinner.

The soldiers asked Mary to tell them about Padre Pio, about his extraordinary gifts. She told them, for example, about the gift of perfume, that at times it was sweet, reminding her of a combination of roses, violets, and lilies, while at other times it was suggestive of disinfectant. The perfume indicated the presence of Padre Pio; it was a sign of grace bestowed by God. Mary told her visitors about Padre Pio's gift of bilocation — his ability to be in two places at the same time but never physically leaving the monastery. She told them of his part in curing the blind, the deaf and dumb, the crippled, people with a wide variety of disorders, about Gemma DiGorgia, a child in Sicily whose blindness was cured, who could now see, but from whom Padre Pio would accept no thanks.

Mary told them of Padre Pio's prophecy that no bomb would fall on San Giovanni Rotondo, and that, indeed, no bombs had fallen; that Padre Pio predicted the building of a Capuchin seminary in his hometown and a seminary there was nearing completion; that a hospital, to be called the "Home for the Relief of Suffering," would be built and that this project was underway but that a great deal of money was still needed (some of the soldiers took home with them the appeal for funds, and money was sent

Mary Pyle lived a life of prayer and voluntary poverty for forty years in her house in San Giovanni Rotondo.

The Capuchin Friary and Seminary which Mary Pyle built in Padre Pio's hometown of Pietrelcina.

Home for the Relief of Suffering Hospital dedicated in 1956 with 300 beds; now a thousand bed hospital.

Padre Pio celebrated Mass outdoors at this make-shift altar during the summers from 1954 to 1959 while the new church of Our Lady of Graces was being built.

Padre Pio pauses to encourage his blind admirer Petruccio Cugino before mounting the monastery stairs.

Mary Pyle engaged in animated conversation with her beloved spiritual director Padre Pio.

Parents of Padre Pio, Orazio Forgione and Mary Josephine Forgione.

Author, Dorothy M. Gaudiose (skirt and white blouse),
Mary Pyle, and Mrs. Helena Russo,
the author's sister in 1962.

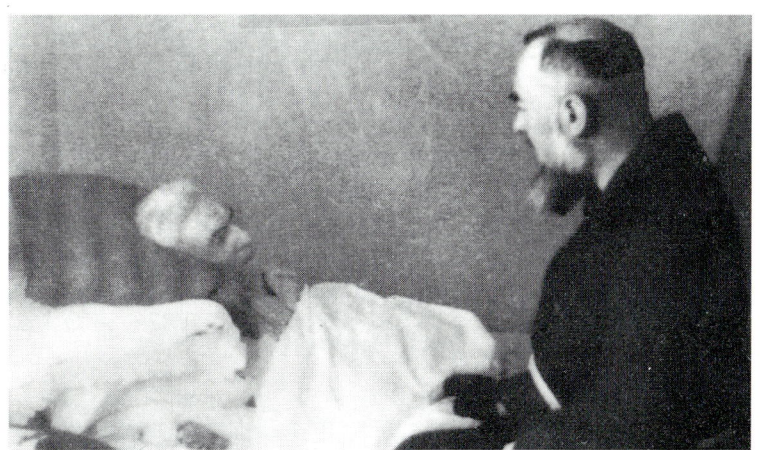

Padre Pio at the bedside of his father, Orazio Forgione, in Mary Pyle's house.

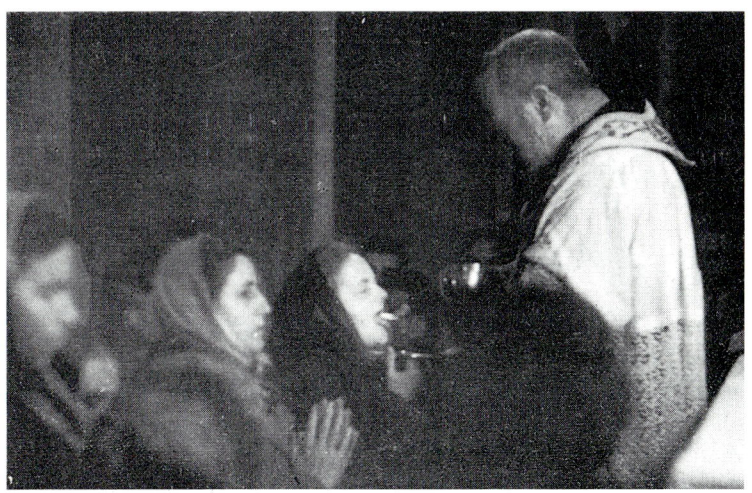

Mary Pyle receiving Holy Communion from Padre Pio in the old 17th century church.

At the end of World War II American soldiers could often be found around Mary Pyle's table.

Members of Mary Pyle's "Missionary Workshop" preparing vestments for priests in Africa.

Mary Pyle as we remembered her in 1962 dressed in the 3rd order Franciscan habit.

Padre Pio often passed Mary Pyle's home (shown here) on his way to or from the monastery.

from people in the United States); that Padre Pio believed that Germany would lose the war, but that Communism would rise; that certain events would occur in the lives of individuals — for example, that Bishop Ursi would become cardinal of Naples (he did). (In subsequent years, Mary received letters from some of the soldiers about whom Padre Pio had made prophecies, for instance, that someone would become a priest or marry or hold a particular professional position.)

Mary told them that, as a confessor, Padre Pio was famous for his ability to persuade a penitent to confess sins Padre Pio wished him to confess. Padre Pio could enumerate the sins a person had committed — how many times he had missed Mass, how many promises he had broken, the mortal and venial sins he had committed but which must not be committed again.

Afterward, Mary might suggest to her soldiers-visitors that they attend Padre Pio's 5:00 a.m. Mass, where they would be edified by the devout celebration of the Mass, and that at the consecration, the wounds in Padre Pio's hands would bleed.

"Could you tell us about Padre Pio's wounds?" asked Joe Peterson, a soldier from Yonkers, New York. "Yes," Mary answered; "but first I should tell you that, when Padre Pio received the stigmata, on September 20, 1918, in the choir of the monastery, it was following the celebration of Mass."

"Then people knew about the stigmata right away?" the soldier asked.

"No; Padre Pio kept them hidden for a week! They were not discovered until a monk who did the laundry reported to the Father Superior the bloodstains on the sheets of Padre Pio's bed, and the Father Superior called Padre Pio to his office to explain the presence of the blood. That is how, under obedience to his superior, Padre Pio came to write what happened."

Mary told them she had a copy of the report by the doctor who examined Padre Pio's wounds, a Dr. Luigi Romanelli. Doctor Romanelli described the wounds as circular with clean-cut borders and having a diameter of little more than two centimeters. The lesions were covered by reddish brown scabs. There was no point at which blood appeared, no edema, no inflammatory reaction in the surrounding tissue. The wounds in Padre Pio's feet have the same characteristics as those in his hands, but are wider at the tip. The scabs on the wounds were produced by drying of the blood that flowed from them.

"The stigmata resemble the five wounds of Christ," Mary told her listeners. From time to time, the scabs fall off and reveal the wounds in great detail. Their contours were so precise that even under a magnifying glass one could see no edema or reddening. When soft, the scabs became detached first from the edges and then from the center, until they fell off in their entirety, making way for the formation of new scab tissue.

Other physicians were sent to examine (and verify) Padre Pio's wounds. The Vatican sent two doctors — Giorgio Festa, a Christian, and Amico Bignami, an atheist. Doctor Bignami was puzzled by the wounds, whereas Doctor Festa described them as wounds similar to those of Christ. The chest wound — about an inch below the left nipple, near the heart — was three quarters of an inch long, with a shallow, tapering line extending from it. The wound was indeed bloody, and it *was* in the shape of an inverted cross. The appearance of the lesion's edge indicated that the wound was not superficial. Though not inflamed, the tissue in the vicinity of the lesion was painful even to the lightest touch. Doctor Festa reported that he had noted a few more drops of blood draining from the chest wound than from the other wounds. According to the monastery's records, Padre Pio lost about a teacupful of blood a day.

Whenever people suggested to Padre Pio that the stigmata were caused by too great a concentration on Christ's passion, he would reply: "Go out to the fields and look closely at a bull. Concentrate with all your might. Do this, and see if horns grow on your head!"

Beginning about three months before Padre Pio's death, the wounds on his body emitted less and less blood until, by the time he died, on September 23, 1968, the five wounds had closed altogether. They had been a part of him for fifty years.

As already mentioned, many of the soldiers Mary had come to know during the war returned to the United States, taking with them her message concerning Padre Pio's desire to build a hospital. When donations began arriving, Mary was given the task of keeping track of and dispensing the money, much of which went toward construction of the hospital.

Acts of Charity

A separate, interesting book could be written on the many facets of Mary's life and activities, so rich and at the same time alien to all appearances of ostentation were they. Mary performed silently many acts of charity, however, always under the auspices of Padre Pio, always the willing disciple in his apostolate. Padre Pio knew his disciple Mary well, too. For example, in 1945, he was visiting the home of the Floria sisters, one of whom was ill, and a group of women from the area, having learned that Padre Pio was there, hastened to be present. As was the custom after prayers and the blessing of the ailing woman, the women lined up, pushing to be among the first to kiss Padre Pio's hand. Meanwhile, Mary Pyle, unassuming as usual, stood at the back of the group. Noticing her, Padre Pio called to her: "Come, Maria; you should be among the first. You have done good for everyone!"

A friend of Mary's who occasionally came for visits told my sister and me that when, in 1939, she first went to San Giovanni Rotondo, it was especially to meet and get to know Padre Pio. Instead, the first person she encountered was Mary Pyle. It was sunset; suddenly, the friend seemed to have developed a headache, probably caused by the bright, warm sun. She and Mary chatted for a few minutes; then the friend turned to complaining about the lack of bath facilities in San Giovanni Rotondo. There was no this or that, she said. All the time she was speaking, Mary said not a word, merely regarding the other woman with such a sweet, beneficent look that the woman quickly realized that Mary had other, more important matters on her mind.

Indeed, San Giovanni Rotondo at that time had no good restaurants and no hotels. Well aware of this, Mary immediately invited her friend to be her house guest, and at that moment the woman realized what Mary Pyle was — a warm, cultured, congenial person. They soon became fast friends, and the woman stayed with Mary for some time. Mary Pyle, the woman continued, not only was the result of an aristocratic upbringing but her behavior and outlook had in some ways been improved by exposure to Padre Pio and by fifteen years' attendance at Padre Pio's "school," an experience that had had a profound influence on Mary.

Father Ezechia Cardone told us of an experience concerning Padre Pio that he had in 1945. While on a visit to San Giovanni Rotondo, Father Ezechia was given a notebook by Padre Pio that contained some handwritten meditations. Later, he loaned the notebook — entitled "The Meditations of Padre Pio, O.F.M." and subtitled "The Agony of Jesus in the Garden" — to Mary, who was immensely pleased with the opportunity to read it. After three days, she returned the notebook to Father Cardone.

About a year later, Father Ezechia was again visiting San Giovanni Rotondo, and Mary asked him for a copy of the notebook for her own use. In addition, she thought, the members of her household would benefit from reading the meditation, especially during the midnight holy hour that was held on Thursdays. Guests in Mary's home were often invited to the meditations, and they, when shown the notebook, were so impressed with it that they wanted copies for themselves. At first, Father Ezechia said, he refused Mary's request, primarily because he did not wish to be censured by Rome, since, at that time, publications by Padre Pio were forbidden. After two years, however, Mary succeeded in getting the ban lifted. Padre Pio was informed of this and, after Mary offered to pay the printing costs, agreed to publication of the meditation.

In this beautiful piece of writing, Padre Pio beseeches the Holy Spirit to enable him to compose a meditation on the Passion of Christ. The meditation is divided into four parts, with each part beginning with a scene of sacred, terrifying drama. The final prayer, a résumé of the divine tragedy, is a petition designed to obtain the corresponding graces, and it closes the meditation. The "Prayer in Conclusion" is as follows.

> *O Jesus, impart to me also that same strength when my weak nature foreseeing future evils, rebels, so that like Thou, I may accept with serene peace and tranquility all the pains and distress which I may meet on this earth of exile. I unite all to Thy merits, to Thy pains, Thy expiations, Thy tears, that I may cooperate with Thee for my salvation and flee from sin, which was the sole cause of making Thee sweat blood and which led Thee to death. Destroy in me everything that does not please Thee, and with the sacred fire of Thy love write Thy sufferings into my heart. Hold me so closely to Thee, with a bond so tight and so sweet, that I shall never again abandon Thee in Thy sufferings.*
>
> *May I be able to rest on Thy Heart to obtain comfort in the sufferings of life. May my spirit have no other desire but to live at Thy side in the Garden and unite itself to the pains of Thy Heart. May my soul be inebriated with Thy blood and feed itself with the bread of Thy sufferings. Amen.*

"Meditation on the Immaculate Conception"

THROUGH Mary's efforts, another meditation was published, entitled "Meditation on the Immaculate Conception," which follows.

Eternal Love, Spirit of Light and Truth, make a way into my poor mind and allow me to penetrate as far as it is possible to a wretched creature like myself, into that abyss of grace, of purity and holiness, that I may acquire a love of God that is continually renewed, a love of God Who, from all eternity, planned the greatest of all the masterpieces created by His hands; the Immaculate Virgin Mary.

From all eternity Almighty God took delight in what was to be the most perfect work of His hands, and anticipated (the) works of His hands, and anticipated this wonderful plan with an outpouring of His grace.

Man, created innocent, fell by disobeying Him; the mark of original sin remained engraved on his forehead and that of his progeny who will bear its consequences until the end of time.

A woman brought ruin, and a woman was to bring salvation. The one, being tempted by a serpent, stamped the mark of sin on the human race, the other was to rise through grace, pure and immaculate. She would crush the head of the serpent (that) was helpless before her and (that) struggled in vain under her heel; for she was conceived without sin, and through her came grace to mankind.

Protected with Grace by Him Who was to be the Savior of Mankind that had fallen into sin, she escaped all shadow of evil. She springs from the mind of God as a pure ray of light, and will shine like a morning star over the human race that turns to her. She will be the sure guide who will direct our steps toward the Divine Son which is Jesus Christ. He makes her radiant with divine splendor and points to her as our model of purity and sanctity. No creature surpasses her, but all creation defers to her through the Grace of Him Who made her immaculate. He whom she was to carry in her womb was the Son of God participating with the Father and the Holy Spirit in the glory of her conception.

Clothed in light from the moment of her conception, she grew in grace and comeliness. After Almighty God, she is the most perfect of creatures; more pure than the angels; God is indeed well pleased (with) her, since she most resembles Him and is the only worthy repository of His secrets.

In the natural order she preceded her Divine Child, our Lord, but in the divine order Jesus, the Divine Son, arose before her, and she received from Him all graces, all purity and all beauty.

All is darkness compared (with) the pure light that renews all creation through Him Whom she bore in her womb, as the dew on the rose.

The Immaculate Conception is the first step in our salvation. Through this singular and unique gift, Mary received a profusion of Divine Grace, and through her cooperation, she became worthy of absorbing infinitely more.

My most pure Mother, my soul so poor, all stained with wretchedness and sin, cries out to your maternal heart. In your goodness, deign, I beseech you, to pour out on me at least a little of the grace that flowed into you with such infinite profusion from the Heart of God. Strengthened and supported by this grace, may I succeed in better loving and serving Almighty God Who filled your heart completely, and Who created the temple of your body from the moment of your Immaculate Conception.

The Three Divine Persons imbue this sublime creature with all her pivileges, her favors and her graces, and with all of her holiness.

The Eternal Father created her pure and immaculate and is well pleased (with) her, for she is the worthy dwelling (place) of His only Son. Through the (generation) of His Son in His bosom from all eternity, He forecasts the generation of His Son as Man in the pure womb of this mother, and He clothes her from her conception in the radiant snowy garment of grace and of most perfect sanctity; she participates in His perfection.

The Son Who chose her for His mother poured His wisdom into her; from the very beginning, by infused knowledge, she knew her God. She loved and served Him in the most perfect manner as He never until then had been loved and served on this earth.

The Holy Spirit poured His love into her, she was the only creature worthy or capable of receiving this love in unlimited measure because no other had sufficient purity to come so near to God; and being near to Him could know and love Him evermore. She was the only creature capable of containing the stream of love which poured into her from on high. She alone was worthy to return to Him from whom came that love. This very love prepared her for that "fiat" (that) delivered the world from the tyranny of the infernal enemy and overshadowed her, the purest of doves, making her pregnant with the Son of God.

Oh, my Mother, how ashamed I feel in your presence, weighed down as I am with faults! You are most pure and immaculate from the moment of your conception, indeed, from the moment in eternity when you were conceived in the mind of God.

Have pity on me! May one compassionate look of yours revive me, purify me and lift me up to God, raising me from the filth of this world that I may go to Him Who created me. Who regenerated me in Holy Baptism, giving me back my white stole of innocence that original sin had so defiled. Dear Mother, make me love Him! Pour into my heart that love that burned in yours for Him. Even though I be clothed in misery, I revere the mystery of your Immaculate Conception, and I ardently (hope) that through it you may purify my heart so that I may love your God and my God. Cleanse my mind that I may reach up to Him, contemplate Him, and adore Him in spirit and in truth. Purify my body that I too may be a tabernacle for Him and be less unworthy of possessing Him when he deigns to come to me in Holy Communion. Amen.

We, too, redeemed by Holy Baptism, are corresponding to the grace of our vocation when, in imitation of our Immaculate Mother, we apply ourselves incessantly to the knowledge of God, in order that we may ever learn better to know Him, to serve Him and to love Him.

Z'Orazio

NEARLY a decade after his wife's death, Z'Orazio (as everyone called him) came to San Giovanni Rotondo to make his home, and for the greater part of the next decade lived in Mary's house, in the room where his wife had died. Z'Orazio kept a photograph of his wife on a dresser in his room; he treasured the picture almost to the point of veneration.

Then, one day, the portrait disappeared! Z'Orazio, greatly upset, clamored for its return. He badgered everyone in the house, until he had upset the routine of the entire household staff. When he was finally told that someone had given the picture to his son, the old man went to Padre Pio and demanded that it be returned.

The old man spent much of his time sitting in the shade of an elm in front of the monastery, where he exchanged stories and anecdotes with various townspeople who stopped by to chat. In an accident that occurred in early 1946, Z'Orazio fell down a steep flight of stairs in Mary's house. By some miracle, he wasn't killed. At one point in his convalescence, he complained to Padre Pio about the pain he suffered. "Instead of complaining," his son replied, "thank your guardian angel who put a pillow on every step!"

Carmela, a member of Mary's household, said that when Padre Pio's father became gravely ill in October 1946, Padre Pio, with the authorization of his superior, came from the monastery to comfort and assist his father and, if necessary, to give him the last sacraments of the Church. Because he himself felt so weak, Padre Pio, accompanied by his superior, Padre Raffaele, stayed in Mary Pyle's house overnight. Holy Communion was brought to him and to his father.

Padre Pio stayed in a small room of the house. Occasionally he wished to rest awhile on the bed in the room but found it so hard that he could neither sleep nor rest for long. "My daughter," he said to Mary, "what a hard bed you have!" And soon, Padre Pio was provided with a softer bed, one with a cotton mattress. The bed, in fact, was the one Mary ordinarily used. Specially made, it consisted of a large wood chest in the shape of a bench. In the chest, Carmela said, were kept out-of-season linens. Over the chest was placed a mattress of horsehair, and underneath, a mattress of wool, to elevate the bed somewhat. Everyone but Mary, it seemed, regarded the bed as being extremely hard — a feature Mary no doubt had in mind when she ordered such a bed.

On October 7, 1946, Orazio, aged eighty-four, died and was buried near his wife in the cemetery of San Giovanni Rotondo. After the burial, some of the brethren of Padre Pio found him grieving. "Have courage," one of them said. Padre Pio lifted his eyes and, in a faltering voice whispered: "It is a father I have lost."

Efforts on Behalf of Padre Pio

IN 1947, near the monastery of San Giovanni Rotondo, construction of the hospital began. Padre Pio had already christened the hospital "Casa Sollievo della Sofferenza" (Home for the Relief of Suffering). "Padre," Mary asked Padre Pio one day, "can I do something for your hospital?" He replied: "You have your work in Pietrelcina. Think about that."

The next year, Mary Pyle returned to New York City, accompanied by Anita Lodi, another Third Order Franciscan. Both women wore the habit of the order. Mary had come to visit an aunt who was dying of cancer and who had left Mary an inheritance. Mary and Anita remained in the United States for four months.

Those who saw Mary Pyle in those days, as well as those who knew her before she renounced her wealth, were sad that she had been reduced to such financial circumstances — all in order to follow in the footsteps of her spiritual director, Padre Pio.

Friends persuaded Mary to speak to various groups about Padre Pio, and she did. By speaking and through other efforts, she raised enough money (including the inheritance from her aunt) to finance the completion of her project of building a monastery in Pietrelcina.

When Mary and Anita returned to San Giovanni Rotondo, she told Padre Pio she had not missed receiving Holy Communion one day during her four-month absence. "Yes," replied Padre Pio, "but then, you have not missed a single day in four years!" It was true, but Mary had never told him that.

The Young Pilgrim

SOMETIME in 1950, a young man appeared in San Giovanni Rotondo, carrying a wooden cross that had been signed with the names of the places and the sanctuaries he had visited, as well as the names of the people he had met. He was on a pilgrimage, he said, and after Mary had given him something to eat, asked her if he might spend the night. Mary was somewhat taken aback by the request, since, at the suggestion of the local police, she allowed only women to stay overnight in her house, it being considered risky for men to do so. This time, however, Mary was inclined to make an exception. "Well," she said to a woman in her household, "it *is* the Holy Year of 1950, and the young man *is* on a pilgrimage. Tomorrow he resumes his journey; so we'll let him stay the night. We can give him a mattress to put on the floor in the kitchen."

That same day, a woman arrived from the United States. After supper she went upstairs for the night but forgot that she had left her purse, containing a great deal of money, in a corner of the kitchen. During the night, the young pilgrim stole the purse and at daybreak, before anyone else was up, left. As one might expect, there was great distress when the theft was discovered. The strange part of the incident was that, instead of keeping the purse and the money, the young man went to the police and demanded that they arrest him, saying. "I am a thief. Arrest me and put me in jail."

In questioning him, the police learned where he had spent the previous night. Later, two policemen took the confessed thief to Mary Pyle's house, where the theft and the identification of the thief were confirmed. The police told Mary that she had been warned against allowing men to stay in her house overnight, that she had no authority to accommodate them, and — worst of all — that she was liable to prosecution or a fine for having done so.

In a manner that was both joking and serious, Mary said to the policemen: "This is ironic. You would free the man who robbed my guest, but you will put in prison the person who has committed an act of charity!"

The young man then returned the money along with the purse. The police asked the American woman if she wished to press charges. "No," she said; "he returned everything he stole; so I will take the matter no further."

"The Cross is a convenient passport for you, young man," Mary said to him. "Leave it here — and now you may leave!" Sometime later it was learned that the young man had committed a burglary in Ravenna. He did indeed profit by misusing the Cross.

Mary's Hospitality

CARMELA, who oversaw the running of Mary's household, told us that, to accommodate her guests, Mary often was left with no place to sleep. For example, a great many people were always present for Padre Pio's anniversaries, and Mary Pyle always gave up her sleeping place to one or another visitor. On one such occasion, Mary went to her room only to find it already occupied and someone asleep in her bed. Rather than waken the person by objecting, she found a chair on which to spend the night, however uncomfortable it was.

On the twenty-fifth anniversary of Padre Pio's ascension to the priesthood, so many people arrived that the hotels and Mary's house were all filled to capacity. From the nearby town of San Marco came a poor, elderly woman who had often been a guest in Mary's house. She was told that no beds were available. "It's not important," she said. "I shall remain here. Get me a mattess and put it on the table, and I will sleep there." Showing no impatience, Mary did as the old woman asked.

A Letter to Carmelita

SOME of the difficulties Mary Pyle encountered living on Gargano Mountain, in San Giovanni Rotondo, are related in a letter she wrote to my sister, Carmelita. This, in part, is what she wrote:

Dearest Carmelita,

I am ashamed to say that I have received all of your letters with generous offerings. I have delivered the offerings — some were for Masses and the Masses will surely have been said, but I must confess that I have not yet spoken to Padre Pio about your problem. However, I intend to speak to him about it if God permits at my next confession, which should be on the 23rd of this month, and I will try to write you his answer at once, so you will probably receive it before this . . . letter reaches you.

My house has (been) turned into a small hospital. Concetella, you may not remember her, but she is one of the younger members of my household, (and she) has been very sick in the hospital. (She) has now returned home but is almost permanently in bed with a very bad heart. Carmela, my dearest little helper and friend, has been very sick in the house, in bed with the flu, and I have been keeping her company. Caterina has been locked in the house for over three weeks because of the snow, and other members of our family (are) in more or less the same condition. At times we have been without light, without heat, and without water, because everything was frozen. I am not trying to excuse myself for not having written, but just want to show you a few of our difficulties.

You probably know that we can only approach Padre Pio when we go every ten days to confession. . . .

Poor old blind Peter does carry messages, but it is not the same. Do not forget to make use of your Guardian Angel, who never fails and is not (hindered) by influenza or snow. I hope that when you receive this, you will already have received your message (with the) answer to your question.

Love and a big paternal blessing from Padre Pio.

Yours,
Mary Pyle

Maria Winowska

IN the summer of 1956, a tall, heavyset woman from Poland arrived in San Giovanni Rotondo. The woman had asked for lodging at all the available hotels, to no avail. It was getting dark, and, feeling discouraged and somewhat melancholy, she decided to go to the church and pray.

As she knelt in prayer, she noticed coming toward her a woman dressed in the habit of a Capuchin. "Good evening,

Madam," the other woman said. Her pronunciation of Italian startled the first woman. *This must be the Mary Pyle that my friends told me about*, she thought. Taking courage, the woman explained her problem: she could not find lodging. Mary Pyle simply asked the woman to follow her. As they walked along, the woman confided to Mary how she felt about not being able to find a place to stay. Laughing, Mary Pyle said: "By chance, I have a room and a second bed that are free."

"Oh, holy Franciscan hospitality," the woman exclaimed. "Behold — I am settled!"

They walked down a steeply pitched road that ran alongside the wall of a cliff, and in a few minutes arrived at a rose-colored house ablaze with lights. They entered a large, noisy room on the first floor, which also served as kitchen and parlor. Mary Pyle introduced the woman to her household: Carmela, Tonina, Catherine, and Maria. "I present to you a friend," she said. "She will spend the night in the house — and, to tell the truth, I do not yet know her name!" As everyone laughed, the new guest introduced herself. She was Maria Winowska, a journalist, and had come to interview Padre Pio. (She later wrote *The True Face of Padre Pio*, a biography that helped introduce Padre Pio to the people of Poland.)

Soon, Maria Winowska, with notebook and pencil in hand, was interviewing Mary on the subject of Padre Pio. "Do you know him well?" she asked. "No one knows Padre Pio *well* — only God." Mary answered. "No one knows his intimate life except, naturally, his confessor; and (his confessor) is not permitted to reveal anything (that is said in confessional). All (the rest of us) can do is gather the crumbs that fall from the table of a king . . . though even the crumbs are precious and are worth gathering."

"But," Maria Winowska continued, "don't you know someone in San Giovanni Rotondo who could tell me what I want to know?"

"Certainly. Look at these houses, at this village. Little by little, they have risen around the monastery. It was built by people who were converted by Padre Pio, by those who received miraculous cures through his intercession, and by his spiritual children. It is not easy to find a man like this — a precious pearl, who, with joy, disposes of all his material wealth, in order to acquire it."

"Each one living near the monastery," Mary said, "can tell you of an experience with Padre Pio. Many of them were fugitives who converted, whose souls were on the brink of hell. Padre Pio has his own special way of dealing with such people. When he interests himself in one of these souls, it is for good; there is no turning back. Once Padre Pio said, 'When I have saved a soul, I never let it fall again!' "

Mary's Generosity

MARY had an abundance of goodness — from which some people profited by asking for loans, even sometimes large amounts that were not repaid. Mary never objected, though; nor did she ever take legal action. She trusted everyone who, in her view, had a true Christian spirit.

Some who were in debt to Mary repaid their loans in cash, some with clothing or other items. Whichever it was, Mary took it and bought clothes for the poor, or made altar cloths for the monastery chapel, or gave to poor children. It did not bother her that she was not always repaid in full. "I prefer to lose even money," she used to say, "than the peace of my soul."

One day, Mary told us, she received a summons to appear at the magistrate's office in San Giovanni Rotondo. Surprised and perplexed, she wondered what the reason might be; nevertheless, at the beginning of the next week, she appeared as directed.

She was dumbstruck when told that she had swindled a certain "E.B." (she would not reveal the name) of three hundred thousand lira (then about two hundred dollars in American currency). Then she remembered that someone whose initials were E.B. had borrowed that amount from her and had made no effort to repay the money. Mary explained to the magistrate the circumstances under which the man had obtained the money. The magistrates listened, then said: "Do not concern yourself about this man. He is well known to the police for cheating and swindling. As for you, the villagers have spoken of the good works you have performed!" Thus was Mary Pyle exonerated.

Mary Pyle was a soul who without realizing it gave off light like a lamp placed on a candelabrum. Who could count the number of poor people who sought her aid? One thinks not only of material poverty but also of the poverty of the soul. "Mary the American" would often accompany the pilgrims who came to San Giovanni Rotondo to pray with Padre Pio. She assisted at his Masses and recited with him the Rosary at the afternoon benediction services.

Another Letter to Carmelita

ALTHOUGH Mary received an ample monthly income, at the end of each month she usually was left with no money and had to ask the friars for help. The following letter confirms this.

Dear Carmelita,

Here comes a big confession, but a confession which proves that you really are near to me. Two days ago, as I was writing this letter, I was a little worried because I needed a certain amount to pay a bill, and (temporarily) I was broke. The Father who has my money ... was not present, and I did not know where to look for that which was lacking to complete the sum I needed. As I was writing, my Carmela was looking over a pile of letters which I had not had the time to open. Imagine my joy and surprise when I found your birthday present for me, which contained exactly the amount I needed. How I would have liked to hug you and thank you with kisses instead of stupid letters. Now let us talk about something far more important. Thank God, Deo gratias! Our beloved Padre Pio is not and has not been ill. He is well in spite of all that he is suffering, and that is not (a) little, and we too are suffering with him and for him. At Easter he did not officiate at the Holy Week services but not because he was ill, as it was reported in the papers all over the world, but because he is under obedience to Rome, who is trying to bring Mont Blanc down to the level of the sea, but (the mountain) continues to tower high above all other mountains and Padre Pio, with all the restrictions, bars, and barriers, seems even greater, ever more saintly, ever more similar to our crucified Lord. Oh, Carmelita, we must love him, to make up for those who do not understand. We must pray without ceasing, hear Masses, offer Communions and say rosaries and get others to do the same. That is the only thing that we can do to help him. It would be impossible to explain all that has been and is still happening; it would take hours and volumes, and it would be useless. It is much better just to concentrate our thoughts on him and to ask our beloved Jesus, and his Mother to take care of him, to protect and guard him.

  Good-bye dear, and thank you! Thank you in Padre Pio's name for all your gifts and offerings from you and your brother. As I have said before, his thanks are expressed in prayer and blessings. Thank You both for all your generosity towards poor undeserving me and thank all the good souls for the Mass offerings. Do not forget to send your Guardian Angel to Padre Pio, and by doing so, you can always be in touch with him and his blessing hand will always be uplifted over your head. Yes, he sends you his blessing now — and often! You're far away, but very near, sister, with love.

Maria Pyle

P.S. *I will send you, God willing, a goodly supply of small photos of our Padre Pio and some little thank-you cards, at least to some of those who have sent Mass offerings. Tell them that their Masses reach the Throne of God just as soon as they give them.*

To Be Near Padre Pio: L'Abbe Toussaint

AS mentioned, Mary Pyle did not provide lodging for men. Thus one day she sent L'Abbe Toussaint, a Belgian priest, to Angela Bevilacqua, wife of the owner of the hotel in which we were staying, with a request that the priest be given a room, adding that he would take his meals at Mary's house. Angela Bevilacqua agreed to the arrangement.

The priest stayed a few days. As he was preparing to leave, Padre Pio said to him: "Stay a little longer here near me!" Thus, L'Abbe Toussaint remained there about a month. He seemed to get along well with Padre Pio, for, when the priest left San Giovanni Rotondo, Padre Pio gave him an autographed copy of a book. The priest left and returned to Belgium.

Months later, L'Abbe Toussaint returned. This time, he was driving a Pullman bus, and with him were his mother, father, and two relatives, plus twenty young seminary students (he was

Mary Pyle: Under the Spiritual Guidance of Padre Pio

director of a college). L'Abbe Toussaint remained with his group for a week, being provided with the same arrangement as on his earlier visit — a room at the hotel and meals at Mary's house. Mary was pleased to have him visit again.

Angela often encountered Mary in church. Whereas others sought places at the front of the church, near Padre Pio, it was Mary's habit to select a remote corner. She was fond of saying: "Just so I see Padre Pio. Even at a distance from him, I am happy!" One Holy Thursday night, Angela was seated next to Mary in front of the sepulchre (which commemorates the burial of Christ). The two women were praying. At some point, Angela noticed that Mary was asleep but did no disturb her. When Mary awoke a few minutes later, Angela, smiling, said: "So you have come here to sleep?" Calmly and with a smile, too, Mary replied: "With the Lord, one always stays well, even if one sleeps in church — just so we are near Him!"

Assisting Youth

AS a proponent of the Montessori educational system, Mary Pyle maintained an interest in helping youth. A direct way to pursue this philanthropic mission was to make possible the construction of a seminary in Pietrelcina, Padre Pio's hometown, and then to make it a flourishing school for training and otherwise preparing candidates for the Capuchin order. Work on the complex was completed on May 19, 1951, the date of the dedication. Thus was fulfilled a prophecy made by Padre Pio years earlier, when, as a young priest living in Pietrelcina, Padre Pio, during an evening walk with Don Salvator Panullo, the parish priest, stopped and, looking toward the spot where the seminary today stands, said: "I hear the song of angels and I smell the rising of incense going before the throne of God. (On) this place a Capuchin monastery will be built."

Padre Pio Celebrates Mass Outdoors

BECAUSE the seventeenth-century church of Saint Mary of the Graces was too small to hold the crowd of worshippers that attended Padre Pio's daily Mass, it was decided that a new, larger church would be built adjoining the original one. During the three months required for construction, Padre Pio celebrated Mass outdoors on the portico of an adjoining building. The following letter is Mary Pyle's account of one such Mass. Again, she was writing to Carmelita.

Dearest Carmelita,

. . . Padre Pio is now celebrating the Mass out of doors in front of the church, and you cannot imagine how beautiful it is. Everybody can see him, and we can . . . hear and follow every word of the Mass, because there is a microphone. It is . . . heavenly, with the fresh morning air and the pinkish ever-changing sky at (a quarter to) five in the morning. I always think of, and miss, Helena and Dorothy just after the Mass; . . . we used to sit together at that time, waiting to see Padre Pio at the two doors before passing on into the church. This morning there were quite a number of patients leaning out the windows of the Casa Sollievo hospital following the Mass. You simply must come to see the hospital . . . it . . . is wonderful, and . . . wonderful things happen there. The Pope himself has declared that Padre Pio is the one and only founder of the hospital, . . . the absolute

"Padrone." Is it not beautiful that the Pope and Padre Pio are working together? I will send you a little magazine with the Pope's telegram, which he sent to Padre Pio on his name day. . . Lots and lots of love from. . .

Yours,
Mary Pyle

A Letter from Mary Pyle

CARMELITA had written to Mary, telling her of the resentment in the family over Dad's will, in which he left the family estate to her and an older brother, James, who lived with their father. Mary's reply was:

Dearest Carmelita, Helena and Dorothy,

Please forgive me for writing (the three of) you a typed letter, but I am like the old woman who lived in a shoe and had so many children she didn't know what to do. Mine are not children, but letters to answer; and as I cannot spank them all soundly and put them to bed, I must find some other remedy. My mail has accumulated to such an extent that I am afraid I will never catch up even if I do write (this) joint letter, . . . but . . . the real reason is that I want to talk to you all together. I think that you know — I hope that you know — I love all three of you, and I cannot bear to think that there is even a little ruffle (of) hard feeling between you. Of course, I know that it is only a little passing cloud, and by the time you receive this letter it will have already passed on, becoming a thing of the past. I don't care a rap who is right and who is wrong; that is none of my business, and of course everybody always thinks they are right and the other wrong.

What should I say about my mother who divided her property in five parts instead of six, just because I became a Catholic? One of my brothers, James, God bless him, tried to fix it up for me, and because of him, I receive what I now receive; but up to this day, I have never been told what the others received. I know that they receive much more than I do, but how much (more)??? Never enough to make up for not becoming a Catholic. Just remember one thing: before Padre Pio gives . . . absolution, he asks whether you are in peace with everybody, and if you cannot say a sincere "yes" you will get a nice little door closed and Padre Pio is already confessing on the other side, before you can put (in) any ifs, buts or becauses. I think that you had better all come over and make peace here and get a big all-embracing blessing (from) our beloved and ever more wonderful Father. Of course, those who have more will be good and generous and help those who have less, and I will have the joy of seeing you all. Do come! And hurry up, because I am getting very old; on Friday I will be 71 years old! I start this letter on Monday, but it is now Friday and I am 71 years old, oldissima!! I can just hear you all saying, "Many happy returns of the day!" And I say "thanks, dear sisters." I owe you all many thank-you letters. I think I have three, if not four, unanswered letters from Carmelita, each containing a very generous donation, etc. I always delivered anything which is to be delivered to Padre Pio, with the name of the donor and the donor's intentions, just as soon as I received the letter. My part all goes to the new church, which we are desperately trying to get ready. I do not dare say "completed" by the 2nd of July, feast of Our Lady of Grace. They had hoped that it would be ready either for the 5th or

25th of May. There still is too much to be done, too much money needed. We hope that it will be beautiful.

I have forced and ruined my nice little typewriter and consequently, it is cutting up all kinds of pranks; but I am going to send it off, I mean this horribly written letter, because I am sure that you will not mind and that you will close your eyes or at least one eye, and overlook all the mistakes and errors and read only the love which is on the lines and between the lines even if they go slipping all over the place.

Our beloved Padre Pio is very tired and has been suffering with earaches. He told one of his spiritual children that it is true that he takes responsibility (for) their souls, but that they also have the reponsibility toward him because they must help him with their prayers. Pray, pray, pray!

I will send you a picture of the past Pope Pius XII with the prayer for his sanctification. He has already performed miracles and given graces. Of course, we still love and venerate him, but we also love and venerate the present Pope John XXIII, who is similar to St. Pius X. As soon as he became Pope, the same evening, he telephoned his blessing to Padre Pio.

There are so many nice stories about him, but I will tell them to you when you come. Remember that I am waiting for you. I send all Padre Pio's blessings if you are at peace . . . otherwise, a good paternal scolding. Whenever you think of me, tell yourselves that I love you very much. I have difficulty in writing because my time is all taken up between church and visitors who want information, (who) want to hear about Padre Pio; so the days simply fly, and I crawl.

> *Lots and lots of love from*
> *Your faraway sister,*
> *Mary Pyle*

Two years later, Helena and I returned to San Giovanni Rotondo, and I had a chance to speak to Padre Pio about the controversy in the family over my father's will. He listened, then asked: "Whose money was it?" "My father's," I answered. "Then it was his to do (with) as he wished!" Padre Pio replied. Later, when I repeated Padre Pio's words to the rest of the family, the bad feeling over the disposition of the will subsided.

A trip to Paris to Study French

THE following letter, written by Mary Pyle to Carmelita, tells of our trip to Paris to study French at the Sorbonne and about the restrictions imposed on Padre Pio.

October 30, 1961

Dearest Carmelita,

I know that you want a letter, but I simply cannot find time to write one, I have received and consigned all *of your offerings, intentions and messages.*

Helena and Dorothy hated to leave San Giovanni Rotondo, but had such a wonderful experience en route, which proved that our beloved Padre Pio was accompanying them and watched over them. In the train a young doctor from Casa Sollievo (Padre Pio's hospital) gave them (the) address of a hotel in Paris near the Sorbonne and very near one of the beautiful churches in Paris, and everybody . . . had said that it was almost impossible to find rooms in Paris.

Pray very hard, dear, because we are all suffering with our beloved Padre. The Pope (John XXIII) says that he loves Padre Pio much more than we do, and so, perhaps, the restrictions are to protect him.

Oh, Carmelita, in our love for him, we must make up for those who do not understand him. We must pray without ceasing, hear Masses, offer Communion, and rosaries, and get others to do the same. That is the only thing we can do to help him. It would be impossible to explain all that has been (happening) and is still happening. It would take hours and volumes, and it would be useless. It is much better just to concentrate our thoughts on him and ask our beloved Jesus and His Mother to take care of him, to protect and guard him.

Good-bye, dear, and thank you in Padre Pio's name for all your gifts. Lots of love from

*Your
Mary Pyle*

News of Graces

MARY Pyle wished to give to posterity not only the words of Padre Pio — both written and spoken — but also news of the numerous graces the Lord had granted to the faithful through Padre Pio's intercession. The material is presented in two thick notebooks written mainly in English though sometimes in French, which make known what Mary could gather and check over. The principal sources of information were the faithful, either in front of the monastery or in Mary's house (which had become something of a cenacle for prayers as well as a hostel for pilgrims). The accounts that follow were given candidly, sincerely, and confidently.

One day in February 1905, while still a seminarian studying philosophy at the Capuchin monastery of Saint Elia a Pianisi, Padre Pio wrote a description of one of his "bilocations:"

Several days ago I had an extraordinary experience. About eleven o'clock in the evening (January 18, 1905), Brother Anastasio and I were in the choir. Suddenly I found myself, at the same time, in the palace of an extremely wealthy family. The master of the house was dying just as his daughter was about to be born.

Then the Blessed Mother appeared and, turning to me, said: "I am entrusting this unborn child to your care and protection. Although she will become a precious jewel, right now she has no form. Shape and polish her. Make her as brilliant as you can, because one day I would like to have her in my Court in heaven."

"How can this be possible?" I replied. "I am only a poor seminarian and don't know whether I will have the joy and good fortune to become a priest. Even if I do, how will I ever be able to take care of this girl, since I will be so far away from here?"

"Do not doubt me," the Blessed Mother admonished. "She will come to you, but first you will find her in the Basilica of Saint Peter in Rome."

Then I found myself back in the choir.

Giovanna Rizzani was born in Udine the night of January 18, 1905, to Leonilde Serraro and the Marquis Giovanni Battista Rizzani.

The (dying) father . . . had been a . . . practicing member of (the) Masonic Order in Udine. As his death grew near, his fellow

Masons (guarded) the palace day and night, to keep any priests from (hearing his confession). A few hours before the master died, his pious wife, tearfully praying beside his bed, saw . . . a Capuchin monk leave the room and disappear down a corridor. . . . Immediately she went after the monk, but he had vanished.

At that moment, sensing the approach of death within the palace, the watchdog tied outside began to howl. Unable to bear the mournful sound, the wife went downstairs to the door, with the intention of letting (the dog) loose. Suddenly, and unexpectedly, with no pain or complications, she gave birth . . . . Only the steward was present to assist her. Afterward, she even had the strength to carry her prematurely born daughter upstairs to her bed.

The steward knew that a priest was trying to pass through the line of Masons guarding the palace outside, in order to hear the master's confession. Using the birth of the child as an excuse, the steward went outside and told the Masons: "You have the right to keep a priest from going to the bedside of my master because he is one of you, but you cannot prevent him from entering to baptize the premature baby that has just been born inside."

The Masons thus permitted the priest to enter the palace, and he went directly to the master's room and there heard the dying man's confession and helped him settle his affairs with Our Lord. A few minute later, while begging God to have mercy on his soul, the man died.

After her husband's death, the widow took her infant daughter to Rome to live with her parents. The little girl grew up never hearing of Padre Pio or learning of the plan that was to guide her life. Although the girl received a good education, her faith was tested in school by some teachers who did not believe in God. To make matters worse, she knew of no priests who were sufficiently versed in theology to answer questions. Then, one summer afternoon in 1922, she went to Saint Peter's to confess, only to discover that no priests were hearing confessions at that time. The custodian told her the church was about to close and suggested that she return the following day, when several priests would be available to hear her confession. If she looked around and still found no priest, the custodian said, she should come back the next day when the priests would be hearing confession.

No sooner had the custodian left than she saw a young Capuchin monk coming toward her. Approaching him, she said: "Father please let me confess to you."

The priest assented, and they entered a confessional on the left side of the Basilica. After making her confession, Giovanna asked the priest if he could clarify a question she had about the mystery of the Holy Trinity.

In simple language that was readily understandable, the monk explained the Holy Trinity. "My daughter," he said, "when a housewife makes bread, what does she use? Three different ingredients: flour, baking powder, and water. She rolls the dough, which has been mixed and formed into a single substance. The dough is one substance. She uses this dough to make three loaves, yet (it is) separate from the other two. From this example we can proceed to God, who is one Being. At the same time, He is three persons, each one equal yet distinct from the other two. God the Father is neither the Son nor the Holy Spirit. The Son is neither the Father nor the Holy Spirit, nor is the Holy Spirit either the Father or the Son. God the Father begets the Son; the Son proceeds from the Father, and the Holy Spirit come from the Father and the Son. They are three individual beings, equal and at the same time distinct. Nevertheless, they are one God only, because the Divine Nature is unique and identical."

Elaborating upon this mystery of faith, the monk was able to clarify the mystery of the Holy Trinity for the girl and to dispel the doubts she had. Leaving the confessional happy, Giovanna waited outside to thank the monk; but he did not emerge, even after several minutes had passed. Eventually, the custodian reappeared and once again said that, because the church was about to close, she must return the next day if she wished to confess. Giovanna replied that she had just finished making her confession, and was only waiting to thank the priest. Pointing to the confessional, she told the custodian that the Capuchin father who had confessed her was still inside. When the custodian went to see for himself who the priest was, he found the confessional empty. "Young lady, there's no one here!"

"But where can he be?" she exclaimed. "I have not moved from this spot, nor have I seen him come out." Bewildered and perturbed, she departed.

During her summer vacation of 1923, Giovanna went with her aunt and a friend to San Giovanni Rotondo to see Padre Pio for the first time. Arriving in the afternoon, they saw that the corridor connecting the sacristy with the interior of the monastery was thronged with people who had come a great distance to see Padre Pio. Despite the crush of people, Giovanna suddenly found herself confronting Padre Pio as he walked down the corridor. Seeming to recognize her, he stopped and peered at her. "I know you," he said; "you were born the day your father died." As was the custom, he gave Giovanna his hand to kiss and blessed her.

The next morning, her aunt, having by this time confessed to Padre Pio, suggested that Giovanna do so, too. So she queued up to confess, and finally her turn came. Padre Pio gave her his blessing, then welcomed her. "My daughter, finally you have come! I have been waiting for you so many years!"

Surprised, Giovanna replied: "Father, you do not even know me. This is the first time I have ever been in San Giovanni Rotondo. Possibly you have mistaken me for someone else."

"No, I have not mistaken you for someone else," he assured her. "You already know me. Don't you remember? Last year, at the Basilica of Saint Peter in Rome, you came up to a Capuchin friar, looking for a confessor. And he confessed you. I was that Capuchin friar."

Giovanna was nonplussed by this explanation for the mysterious appearance and disappearance of the Capuchin confessor at the Basilica (Padre Pio had gone there in bilocation, just as the Blessed Mother had predicted years earlier when she told him that his spiritual daughter would come to him in Saint Peter's).

"Listen, my daughter," Padre Pio said. "Just before you were born, the Blessed Mother took me to your home, and I witnessed the death of your father. She indicated that through Her intercession and the merits of his wife's tears and prayers, he had obtained salvation. After telling me to pray for him, Our Lady informed me that his wife was about to give birth to a baby girl and that she was placing this child under my care. My daughter," Padre Pio concluded, "you are that child. You are my responsibility."

Filled with emotion, Giovanna began to cry.

"Since I have become your responsibility, Father, please tell me how I should lead my life. Should I become a nun?"

Mary Pyle: Under the Spiritual Guidance of Padre Pio

"No, you should not. Come to San Giovanni Rotondo frequently. I will guide your soul, and you will live according to the will of God."

After receiving Padre Pio's blessing, Giovanna left the confessional with tears in her eyes. Her aunt asked why she had taken so long, and why she was crying, but Giovanna said nothing; she kept to herself what Padre Pio had told her.

Later, as Padre Pio invested her in the Third Order of Saint Francis, he suggested that Giovanna take the name Jacopa. After mildly objecting that the name lacked a pleasant ring, Giovanna asked if she might not be called Sister Clare instead.

"No, you shall be called Sister Jacopa," Padre Pio insisted. "Have you read the life of Saint Francis of Assisi? At one point in the biography there appears a noble Roman lady named Jacopa de Settesoli, whom Saint Francis called 'the beloved mother of our order' in reference to her generosity toward and protection of the Franciscans. Just as she received the grace of witnessing the death of Saint Francis, you, Jacopa, will be present when I die."

The final part of the story is not in Mary's notebook (her death preceded that of Padre Pio by five months); nevertheless, I think it fitting that this reminiscence conclude with it.

Under Padre Pio's spiritual guidance, Giovanna continued in her virtuous ways, developing into a lovely, pious lady. She married the Marquis of Boschi and they raised a beautiful Christian family. Although Giovanna frequently went to San Giovanni Rotondo to visit her spiritual father, for some months during the last year of his life, she was unable to do so.

One day, she heard Padre Pio's calm, sweet voice. "Come soon to San Giovanni Rotondo, because I am going away. If you take too long you will miss me."

By this time, Giovanna too was elderly. Still, with a friend, she hurried to San Giovanni Rotondo to be at Padre Pio's side. Four days before his death, she had the good fortune to confess to him. When Padre Pio saw her, he said: "Because this will be the last time you will confess to me, I absolve you now of all the sins you have ever committed."

"Why is that, Father? Why can't you confess me anymore?"

"I have already told you. I cannot confess you because I am going away."

At that point, Giovanna realized that Padre Pio was telling her that he was dying and would soon be gone.

Padre Pio's Last Blessing

ON the evening of September 22, 1968, Padre Pio gave his last blessing to the thousands of his spiritual children who had come from around the world to visit him on the fiftieth anniversary of his stigmata. After the blessing, he retired to his cell; at that time, Giovanna found herself present in spirit in Padre Pio's cell to witness in detail the last hours of the life of her spiritual father — just as he had predicted she would years earlier when, at his suggestion, she took the name Sister Jacopa. She saw him suffer and pray, and watched as he confessed with Padre Pio Pellegrino, renewing his religious vows. Giovanna saw Padre Pio taken from his bed to the veranda, where three physicians ministered to him. Finally, she was an observer as Padre Pio received the last rites of the Church. As she saw him die, Giovanna cried: "Padre Pio is dead! He is dead!"

Giovanna's cries awakened her friend and numerous guests at the hotel as well. Her friends tried to calm Giovanna, telling her that she was having a bad dream; but Giovanna insisted that wasn't so, and she quickly dressed and hurried to the monastery. A small crowd had already gathered in the square before the church, and a Capuchin friar was at that moment officially announcing the death of Padre Pio.

A few days later, Giovanna told a Capuchin friar that she had witnessed the death of Padre Pio. At first, he did not believe her. Seeking to convince him, she said: "Padre, I will describe Padre Pio's room as I saw it when he lay dying. Maybe that will convince you." (Padre Pio's room had never before been photographed, nor had a woman been permitted to enter it.) "Enough," the friar exclaimed. "I believe you when you say you were present at Padre Pio's death."

Many were so surprised at Padre Pio's utterances to them, Mary Pyle said, that they later would tell her what he had said and done. One day she told us what had been related to her about Padre Pio on the subject of abortion. One morning, Mary met a distinguished-looking woman who asked Mary to pray for her. The woman was accompanied by two of her daughters, one fourteen years old and the other four. The older daughter was deaf and dumb, but the younger one was normal. The woman had left her other two children at home — a girl and a boy, both deaf and dumb.

Between spells of sobbing, the woman told Mary why she was there. On her third pregnancy, when she already had two deaf and dumb daughters and was feeling the same symptoms she had experienced during her first two pregnancies, she feared that the third would also be born deaf and dumb. Both she and her husband felt that they would not be able to stand the suffering of seeing most of their children deaf and dumb.

The struggle was great, but finally, with her husband's consent, the woman made the decision to have an abortion. From that moment on, she had no peace. The woman went to confession. The priest who heard her confession, after sharply rebuking her, extracted a promise from her that she would do no such thing again, and absolved her. Still, she did not feel calm. As her unease continued, she decided to go to Padre Pio.

With trepidation she approached Padre Pio's confessional. He had no sooner opened the shutter than he shouted at her: "Assassin! You have murdered your child!" And he closed the shutter of the confessional and left.

Pierced by suffering, the woman returned home and told her husband everything that had occurred. They were both distraught and spent several days wondering what they had done and about what they had been told.

The woman became pregnant again. This time a boy was born; and he too was deaf and dumb. The woman returned to San Giovanni Rotondo. In the confessional, Padre Pio said to her only these words: "Do God's will."

The woman had still another child. This one was a beautiful little girl. Padre Pio, after blessing the oldest of the woman's daughters, placed his hand on the newborn girl's head and, looking into the mother's eyes, said: "You see what comes of doing God's will? This little girl will always be good, beautiful, clever. She will always remain beside her mother."

Eight Stories from Mary's Notebook

THE following stories are from Mary Pyle's notebook. The titles given are as they appear there.

GIOVANNI DA PRATO

Giovanni da Prato, as he was called (Prato was the name of the town in Tuscany from which he came), was a taxi driver. He was a communist, with a tendency towards violence and drunkenness. When he got drunk, he would beat up his wife.

One night he staggerd into their bedroom and flung himself on the bed. He felt the bed shake, and looking down, saw to his amazement, a Capuchin friar grasping the bed rail and glowering at him. The friar told Giovanni in no uncertain terms what he thought of him and his behavior — then suddenly no longer seemed to be there.

Giovanni leaped out of bed and quickly locked the front door. Then, going into the kitchen, he said loudly to his wife: "Now, then, where's that so-and-so monk?" Brushing aside her protests and denials, he searched the house but could find no one. Gradually he became sober enough to believe his wife.

When she heard from her husband what had happened in their bedroom, the poor woman immediately concluded that there was only one explanation. For some time she had been praying for Padre Pio's help. She had also heard of his ability to achieve bilocation. Was it possible that this was Padre Pio's answer? If it was not, what other explanation was there? "It was Padre Pio," she exclaimed, and in her exultation, her husband's scoffing and curses ran off her like water off a duck's back.

"Look," Giovanni said, "no priest makes a monkey out of me. I will go have a look at this Padre Pio. I will hear what he himself has to say. And, while I am at it, I will find out if he flies!" True to his word, Giovanni got in his taxi and drove to San Giovanni Rotondo. There he found Padre Pio, who spoke to him and led Giovanni to the confessional. "What I forgot," Giovanni said later, "he recalled for me." Eventually, Giovanni took out his card of membership in the Communist party and asked Padre Pio to destroy it. "Yes, I shall," Padre Pio replied. "But you have another card in a drawer of the chest by your bed at home. Destroy that, too, when you return."

Giovanni was more than impressed; psychologically, he was put to rights; he was comforted and consoled as well. Padre Pio promised to remain at his side, if only in spirit, and to help him. Now, before the acts of contrition and the absolution came the payoff. "You have caused a great scandal," Padre Pio said. "Now you must do something to atone for your actions. For your penance you will go every Sunday to Holy Communion at the last Mass in the main church. Do this until I tell you to stop."

At that time there was no relaxing of the rules for fasting or for evening Mass. Those attending Communion did so at an earlier Mass. No one ever went to Communion at the last or the midday Mass. Each Sunday, though, to the amazement and whispered comments of the worshippers in the congregation, the unhappy Giovanni marched down the aisle, until everyone had become familiar with the practice. The attention of the priest celebrating the Mass frequently had to be drawn to the solitary figure kneeling at the altar rail.

Although Giovanni's penance lasted more than six months, during that time he never asked to be released from his obligation. Furthermore, he challenged those who doubted his changed outlook and his new activities to meet Padre Pio and decide for themselves. Giovanni did something else as well: He brought groups of his former colleagues to San Giovanni Rotondo to talk with Padre Pio. Over several months, "Giovanni's squad" became a familiar sight in the town. His communist friends were always impressed, so impressed that many were converted.

THE TICKET

Once, when Padre Pio was ill, a friar brought him a stack of envelopes and packages the senders wanted Padre Pio to bless. "Will you bless these, Padre?" the friar asked. Padre Pio looked over the items and replied: "Yes, but not *that* envelope."

A group of people waited at the end of the corridor leading to Padre Pio's room. In due time, the friar emerged from the room and came down the corridor. To the rightful owners gathered, the friar returned an envelope or a package, as appropriate. Finally, only the envelope Padre Pio had rejected was left. "Whose is this?" asked the friar.

"Mine." It was a man who spoke with a strong Neapolitan accent.

"Padre Pio refuses to bless the envelope," the friar said.

There was sensation in the audience — except for one person. "Ah, well," the owner of the envelope finally said, taking back the envelope and grinning sheepishly. "One can only try." He removed a small piece of paper from the envelope and held it up for all to see. It was a coupon for that week's football pool!

LOVE OF GOD

"Padre Pio," a woman said to him one day, "I am ashamed to tell you this, but I believe that I love you more than I love God!"

"I understand. Very well. Then you will do as I say. I want you to go to the village and steal something. Do that for me."

Shocked, the woman replied: "Padre Pio, what are you saying? You know I cannot do that!"

Sternly, Padre Pio continued: "I meant what I said. Go to the village and steal!"

"No, no, Padre. I do not want to steal. It is wrong."

When he had repeated the command the third time, and the woman continued to insist that it was wrong to steal, Padre Pio smiled. "Do you not see?" he asked. When I commanded you to do something contrary to the law of God, you refused to obey me. Therefore, you love God more than you love me. You love me because I lead you to God. If I did not lead you to God, you would no longer love me!"

At this answer, the woman smiled and breathed a sigh of relief.

A CURE

Shortly after the end of World War II, a young wheat farmer had a serious accident, from which he suffered a double embolism, one on each lung. The farmer was taken to the hospital and given various drugs, some of them new and untested. For awhile, they seemed to work; but eventually the embolisms not only remained, they worsened. The young farmer then realized that he was dying. He was young and strong and did not want to die just yet. Therefore, being intelligent and of a religious nature, he prayed to God, asking Him to let someone intercede in his behalf.

That night while the farmer slept, a bearded monk appeared at his bedside. The monk bent forward and laid his hand on the farmer's chest. Then he smiled and disappeared.

The farmer felt better immediately. In fact, to the amazement of his physician, he seemed cured. The farmer told no one except his mother of the apparition, believing that people would think he was neurotic, or worse, that he was deranged. He and his mother kept the secret, leaving the young man's physician and the doctors he called in to their hypotheses. The farmer and his mother concluded that the monk must have once been a great saint.

Several months passed. One day, the farmer was in Padua to sell his wheat. Upon concluding his business with a customer, he was invited to the customer's home for lunch, and accepted. As they entered the living room of the man's house, the farmer was transfixed. There, on the wall, was a photograph of the monk who had appeared to him the night he was ill and dying. He asked his host who the monk was, and the other man replied — Padre Pio.

That evening, the farmer was on a train to Foggia. He arrived at about four in the morning, and from there took a taxi to San Giovanni Rotondo, arriving just in time for Padre Pio's dawn Mass. When the young farmer saw Padre Pio come to the altar, whatever doubts he may have had were dispelled. *Here was the monk who had appeared to him.* It was midwinter and the usual warm-weather crowds had not yet descended on the town; thus he was able to go to confession that same day. He made his confession, and Padre Pio blessed him. "And tell me," Padre Pio said in a quiet, natural voice, "what about the lungs now? How are they?"

"Thank you, Father," said the farmer; "they are fine."

"Have you had them X-rayed?"

"Yes, Father."

"Good. Thanks be to God — and God bless you."

"I assure you," the narrator concluded; "I re-live the emotions of those moments every time I think about it!"

COUNTESS LUISA VAIRO

Countess Luisa Vairo was a London aristocrat — beautiful, elegant, intellectual — who believed in always having new experiences. As curious and capricious as she was, though, one day Luisa found herself at Padre Pio's monastery, kneeling at his feet in the confessional. She was undergoing a crisis of conscience and had hardly begun to speak when Padre Pio allowed her, in her mind's eye, to see a day-by-day film of her life and helped her recall mentally the details she had forgotten to mention.

Luisa emerged from the confessional transformed. She postponed her return to London in order to remain near the monastery. She had repented and now prayed for the transformation of her only son, who led an unfocused life similar to her own.

Near the monastery one morning, Luisa purchased a newspaper and in it read that the ship carrying her son had shipwrecked, with many injured and fifteen dead. She uttered a scream that was heard inside the chapel of the monastery. A minute or two later, Padre Pio came out to see what the matter was. "Who said your son is dead? And why such desperation?" he asked.

"Who will assure me that my son is alive?" Luisa answered, her eyes filled with tears.

To the amazement of everyone present, Padre Pio said: "Thank God. Your son lives. Here is where you can reach him."

Luisa wrote immediately to the address Padre Pio had mentioned and received from her son confirmation of what Padre Pio had said. Everything her son wrote her corresponded to his words.

THE BLIND MAN

A young woman living in an area near San Giovanni Rotondo had heard of the numerous cures effected through Padre Pio's intercession and came to Padre Pio, asking him to intercede on behalf of her husband who gradually had become totally blind. Padre Pio told her that her husband's loss of sight was a punishment by God because once the woman's husband had beaten his father!

The woman could hardly believe this. When she returned home, however, she told her husband what Padre Pio had said. At first he denied that he had beaten his father; then, recalling the past, the husband remembered that when he was about sixteen, he had had an argument with his father and was so angry with him that he beat him severely with an iron rod.

THE TRINITARIAN PADRE PIO

After the Russian Revolution, a young aristocrat had come to Rome, where he became a Roman Catholic. A sculptor and a musician, the cultured young man spoke several languages. Eventually, he came to San Giovanni Rotondo to see Padre Pio. What the young man felt was more than enthusiasm; it was a reconversion or at least a continuation of his conversion. What he had was insufficient; he hungered for more. He felt he had a vocation, but for what wasn't clear, and he asked for Padre Pio's advice. Should he become a priest or a monk, and, if so, in what order? Padre Pio told the young man to return to Rome and pray, that he too would pray that the Lord would give him guidance. The young man obeyed, returning to Rome, where he spent hours praying before Our Lord in the Blessed Sacrament. One day he saw two hands come out of the tabernacle. They were holding a white habit on which was a red and blue cross. Was he awake, or dreaming? The hands still held the white habit, and they were still moving toward him. Then they disappeared.

The young man went to his confessor and told what he had seen. Very interested, the priest told him of the Trinitarians, a religious order whose members wear a habit adorned with a cross of red and blue, and introduced him to the superior of the order. Since the order's habit matched precisely the one the young man had seen, he could only conclude that the Lord had given him a sign, and at once he asked to be received into the order. He was accepted and took the name Pio. He made rapid progress in his studies and was well on the "way to perfection." In due time he was ordained. A short time later, owing largely to his cultural background, training, and knowledge of languages, he was sent to Canada as a parish priest.

When he had been in Canada several years, he wrote a letter to the Vinciguerra family. Mary Pyle said she read his letter, written in 1927. In the letter the priest told about his work, saying: "They almost attribute to me the gift of performing miracles, but they do not know that when I am beside the bed of a (sick or) dying person who needs to be saved, I go in spirit to the little white church on the mountainside, and kneel down at the feet of the humble Capuchin monk, Padre Pio; it is he who converts the dying sinner. It is he who heals the sick person." Thus, said Mary, the two Padre Pio's worked together.

THE WOMAN WHO FELL UNDER THE WEIGHT OF THE CROSS

A family in the town of San Giovanni Rotondo bore the nickname "Tampa-Tampa." The family was poor. Of the three sons, two were Capuchin fathers and the third — young and good-looking — had gone to Abyssinia to find work. When the mother received the news that this son had died there, she was grief-stricken; she could not resign herself to her son's death.

Shortly after she received the sad news, there was a customary fiesta in the town, in which Our Lady of Sorrows was carried through the town. As the procession neared the house where the Tampa-Tampa family lived, the sorrowing mother was unable to contain her grief. Instead of humbly asking help of Our Lady, she ran out into the crowded street and blasphemed Our Lord and Our Lady in a scandalous manner.

In another instance of providence, one of the woman's other sons came home for a few days' visit. He was very sad to find his mother both poverty and grief-stricken, and ill with heart disease, an ailment that could carry her off at any moment. The son went to the monastery and there begged Padre Pio to pray for his mother — above all, to pray that she might die in God's grace.

Days and weeks passed. Finally, one morning, the woman dragged herself slowly up the road to the monastery. She was exhausted when she arrived. She told Mary (who met the woman outside the church) that she had come because she wanted to open her heart to Padre Pio. Mary took her to Padre Pio, and she confessed at length to him, face to face, under the arch in the church where Padre Pio confessed the deaf, the crippled, and the aged who could not kneel at the confessional.

The intense silence of the church was interrupted by the woman's laments and sobbing as she poured out her woes and admitted her sins. Many of those in the church knew what had happened at the fiesta; they thanked the Lord that her soul was returning to the state of grace, and accompanied her confession with their prayers. When the confession ended (it was much longer than usual), Padre Pio passed through the church to the confessional, where numerous penitents awaited him. His face was paler than usual, and his eyes expressed infinite grief, compassion, and love.

The woman received Holy Communion. Later, outside the church, she said she was so tired that she had begged Padre Pio to tell the Lord to call her. He said she must suffer awhile longer. By this time, the woman was so nearly exhausted that she could hardly stand; it would have been impossible for her to walk back to the town. Fortunately, a car was waiting in front of the church, and she was put in it and accompanied to her house, where her daughter answered the door. "Put me on the bed," she said to her daughter, "and call all my children, because Padre Pio has given me grace." A priest arrived and administered Extreme Unction. One last time, the mother looked affectionately at her children gathered around her bed. Then she closed her tired eyes and reposed in peace.

MONSIGNOR DAMINI

Among the letters Mary received one day was a letter from Signora Victor Damini, widow of the famous opera singer from Buenos Aires. In the letter Signora Damini wished to thank Padre Pio for his words of consolation at the time of her husband's death. When she had visited Padre Pio with her husband, Signora Damini had told Mary privately that she would have preferred to stay at home rather than accompany her husband on his concert tours. But, she said, "If I hadn't been standing beside him after his concerts, some other woman would!"

"That reminds me," Mary continued, "I want to tell you about Monsignor Damini, the brother of Signora Damini's husband." And she related the following story.

Monsignor Damini, vicar general of Salto, Uruguay, placed great faith in Padre Pio and had come to visit him. Because of his ecclesiastical position he stayed at the monastery. Monsignor Damini had a weak heart, and one day, while Padre Pio was confessing penitents in the church, Monsignor Damini suffered a heart attack. He begged those tending him to inform Padre Pio at once. This was done, but without effect; Padre Pio had acknowledged the message and continued his confessing. By the time he reached the Monsignor's bedside, the attack was over. When the sick man reproached Padre Pio for not coming earlier, Padre Pio told him he knew it had not been necessary, that the heart attack would not be fatal. "Ah, how I wish I could remain here and be assisted by you on my deathbed," Monsignor Damini said. "Do not worry," was the response; "I shall assist you wherever you are — and you will die in Uruguay!"

The vicar general returned to his diocese and, of course, related the episode to his intimates and to the bishop.

About seven years later, a Capuchin archbishop and other bishops of Uruguay, together with the Papal Nuncio, met in Salto, Uruguay, to discuss a regional seminary. The bishops stayed at the episcopal residence, where Monsignor Damini, as vicar general, had his residence.

One night, the archbishop was awakened by knocking at his door. After struggling to awaken, he noticed that his door was partway open, and past it, he could see a Capuchin monk. The archbishop could not see the monk's face, however. Then a voice urged him to hurry to Monsignor Damini's room, that he was dying. The archbishop got up, put on his cassock, and went for the holy oils. Soon he was hurrying to Monsignor Damini's room. As he went along, he stopped at the doors of the other visiting bishops and alerted them. When he reached Monsignor Damini's room, the archbishop found that, indeed, the man was dying. Soon all ten bishops were gathered, and they gave the monsignor their final blessing. The bishops stayed until Monsignor Damini had breathed his last. Almost immediately after this occurred, the archbishop found a slip of paper on which the monsignor had written the words "Padre Pio came!"

Later, when the Capuchin archbishop came to San Giovanni Rotondo, he confirmed Padre Pio's visit to the monsignor's room in Uruguay. This, Mary asserted, clearly was a case of bilocation, the ability to be in two places at the same time.

Pio Abresch

ONE morning, as I was working with Mary Pyle, I told her that I had found the best pictures of Padre Pio at Abresch's (a photography studio on the main thoroughfare, near the hotel where I was staying). I asked Mary what nationality Mr. Abresch was. Frederico Abresch, she said, was a German who had married an Italian woman. At the time of their marriage, Frederico, a Lutheran, had converted to Catholicism. The couple made their home in Bologna, where Frederico worked as a photographer.

When they had been living there for some time, Mrs. Abresch became seriously ill, and a friend of theirs suggested to Frederico that he take his wife to Padre Pio in San Giovanni Rotondo. Mrs. Abresch's physician had diagnosed her illness as a tumor and had recommended surgery. When told this, Padre Pio said that she was with child and that she should prepare for a birth.

Frederico and his wife returned to Bologna. They did not know what to do, however. Padre Pio, via bilocation, appeared to Mrs. Abresch and again told her to prepare for the birth. It would be a boy and should be called Pio. Finally, Padre Pio told them, the boy would become a priest. Soon, a boy was safely delivered.

In gratitude to Padre Pio, Frederico Abresch took his wife and newborn son to San Giovanni Rotondo to live. As the boy grew up there, he often served Padre Pio's Mass. One morning, Padre Pio put his hand on young Pio Abresch's head and said: "Someday you will hold high office in the Church." Those who heard about the prediction thought it meant that Pio Abresch would someday be either a pope or a cardinal, and thus they came to view the boy in a new light.

No more children were born to the Abresches. Today, Pio Abresch is a priest serving in the Vatican, and both of his parents have passed on. The studio photography shop still bears the Abresch name but is under new management.

Fair Share

MARY told my sister and me another story, this one about an industrialist. One day, the industrialist, who was from northern Italy, came to visit Mary. He was accompanied by an attractive woman whom he introduced as the overseer of his household. The industrialist asked Mary if his companion might stay with her while he went to talk to Padre Pio, and Mary agreed.

Sometime later, the man returned. As he and his woman companion were leaving, he said that Padre Pio had been so kind and gracious to him that he had decided to confess to him the next day. The next evening, when the man returned alone to visit with Mary, he told her that he was so impressed with Padre Pio's advice that he wished to share it with her. He had come to see Padre Pio at the insistence of his wife. The woman who was with him earlier was more to him than the overseer of his household; she was his mistress. Mary said she was somewhat surprised to hear that. Be that as it may, the industrialist said, he actually had wanted to give half of his estate to his wife and family and the other half to the Franciscans. "Yes," Padre Pio had told him; "but I want you to do it in the following manner. Allot one-third of the estate to your wife and family, one-third to the Franciscan order, and one-third to your mistress. You will recall that when, as a young girl, your mistress came to work for you, that you provided her with many luxuries that she did not know about. Now, under your patronage, she has become accustomed to them. If you do not provide them for her, she will go out and sin so that she will not again be without those luxuries. When you return home, arrange your affairs thus.''

The industrialist admitted that he had never thought about it in that way.

Six months later, Mary continued, she received a letter from the man's wife, telling Mary that her husband had followed the instructions given him by Padre Pio. Five months after his visit to San Giovanni Rotondo, her husband had died of cancer.

In view of the fact that, through the mistress, a second family was involved, Padre Pio recommended that the man pay for the education of these children, that he leave his mistress and return to his wife.

Gian Battista

THE story of an encounter between Mary Pyle and Gian Battista, a Capuchin priest from Sicily, provides insight into her personality.

Father Gian Battista told us that he first met Mary Pyle in 1937 during his first visit to Padre Pio, soon after Father Gian had been ordained. Mary received him cordially and openly, as well as somewhat maternally. He noticed that she displayed great respect, even veneration, towards a priest. Her carriage was upright, and she was dignified and courteous — typical of a woman of great beauty and upper-class upbringing. A member of an upper-class

American family, she nevertheless dressed humbly in the Third Order Franciscan habit.

When he entered that rose-colored house for the first time, he said, he found Mary Pyle seated at the head of a long table. She was stuffing envelopes with printed matter destined for various cities and countries around the world. It was useful work, not only for the benefit of all but in a special way of great benefit to the Franciscan family. She had an active intelligence, innocent eyes, a vivacious welcoming smile, and an outgoing personality — combined with a knowledge of five languages, which was always at the service of Padre Pio.

In 1937, the house Father Gian found amid the squalor of the bare mountain that protected the monastery was the house of "Mary the American." Only in the vicinity of her house could one see flowers and almond trees; otherwise, the area appeared rough and uncultivated. From Foggio to San Giovanni Rotondo, and from there to the monastery, a desolate spectacle of rocks presented itself. During those three happy days that he spent beside Padre Pio, Father Gian took his meals at Mary's house. It was a simple house, of genuine Franciscan style, where nothing was ostentatious or miserly.

In speaking of his nine visits to Padre Pio, Father Gian said that a stop at Mary's house was always obligatory. He took pleasure in noting that, because she spoke their language, every stranger entering her house immediately felt at ease with her. When many different nationalities were represented, as sometimes happened, Mary passed easily from Italian to French to German to English. No one need feel embarrassed at not knowing another language. She granted to all the privilege of listening, of not feeling neglected.

The Beneficial Effect of Padre Pio's Ministry

TO the great range of visitors to San Giovanni Rotondo, Mary Pyle was most careful to present the spiritual profile of Padre Pio and, above all, to give a balanced evaluation of the impact of his ministry. She admired his profound humility. This was manifested by a large painting of him which she kept in her bedroom. It portrays Padre Pio as a young stigmatist in the monastery garden. In it, one of his hands is placed on the other; head is down; and his chin almost rests on his breast. Overall, there is a look of bewilderment and humiliation.

Mary Pyle and Her Franciscan Family

MARY Pyle gathered around herself a "Franciscan family," good women who were engaged in the work of the monastery and the house. She enjoyed — and deservedly so — the full confidence of the Capuchin fathers of San Giovanni Rotondo; and she neither asked for a title for her work nor abused the privilege. For more than forty years she worked for Padre Pio's monastery and for the numerous Franciscan activities in Italy and abroad.

Mary venerated priests profoundly. The proofs of this is in her great compassion for those priests with defects. She prayed and sacrificed for them — always with the goal of being worthy to be received and blessed by Christ. If it is said that priests were the pupil of her eye, and if the phrase seems trite, it is because it was Mary Pyle who said so.

Before the main thoroughfare of San Giovanni Rotondo,

known as the Avenue of the Capuchins, priests and missionaries took their meals at Mary's house and were given lodging. She was no less generous after the hotels were built along the avenues, continuing in her generosity throughout her life.

Her spiritual sensitivity to those who were consecrated to God reached a high degree. She was happy whenever the Capuchins came to visit, saying to every one of them, "I remember Padre Pio; I live for him."

Father Gian continued. The day of July 11, 1962 approached. It was the twenty-fifth anniversary of his ordination, and he had decided to spend it near his beloved Padre Pio. There, he left everything — parish, family, friends in Sicily — and went to San Giovanni Rotondo.

Mary Pyle was deeply touched by his decision. It pleased Padre Pio, too. Through the generosity of Father Rosario of Aliminusa, the father superior, it was decided that not only would Father Gian celebrate Mass in the presence of Padre Pio; he was to have a solemn High Mass with assistants and a choir.

On the day of the twenty-fifth aniversary, to his great surprise and emotion, Father Gian found the major altar of the basilica richly decorated with white flowers and sumptuously illuminated. There were two assistants, a deacon and a subdeacon, and several altar boys.

After the Mass, another surprise, this one at Mary's house — a banquet table decorated for a feast, including beautiful flowers. On Father Gian's right was seated the deacon, and on his left the subdeacon who had assisted him at Mass. The elaborate dinner concluded with cake, ice cream, and coffee. And if that weren't enough, Mary gave Father Gian an envelope with two twenty-dollar bills and a card conveying her congratulations.

After the beauty of that blessed day spent with Padre Pio and Mary Pyle, Father Gian said, he had no regrets about leaving Sicily. To be able to spend the twenty-fifth anniversary of his ordination into the priesthood in San Giovanni Rotondo made it all worthwhile.

Mary Pyle was devoted to the Capuchin fathers, which is understandable, since, for more than forty years, she had worked with and for them. As youngsters, many of the fathers had been encouraged in their studies and helped financially by Mary; to them, she was a mother and was loved as one.

Mary was also a spiritual daughter, the one who most closely resembled Padre Pio in having assimilated his counsel, admonishment, and teaching and put them to good use. She let herself be taught and molded in the hands of the spiritual artist Padre Pio, who found in this creature the precious spirit of an authentic mystic, a true follower of Saint Francis of Assisi, one who had left the world to live solely for God.

Padre Pio's "Spiritual Daughter"

THE relationship of Mary Pyle to Padre Pio, of spiritual daughter to spiritual director, is reminiscent of the relationship of Francis and Clare of Assisi.

The comparison, however, is not altogether accurate; for Mary suffered from the resentment of those near Padre Pio who, like him, were sometimes harsh in their statements and behavior and who did not always explain their reasons for behaving thus. Once, Mary said, Padre Pio asked her — as penance — not to receive Holy Communion for a week. In her eyes, this was a severe form of penance. In explaining Padre Pio's actions, Mary compared him to a great teacher, a great educator who stimulates the soul in order to achieve a certain effect. When the effect has been achieved, Padre Pio withdrew — again, in his own particular way. Every inclination to jealousy or greed — all bad impulses of the soul — was purified, corrected, and molded so that it would be more pleasing to God!

Mary Pyle's Faith in the Honesty of People

MARY Pyle consistently kept her faith in the honesty of people. She seemed incapable of suspecting or believing malice or bad faith on their part. On more than one occasion, Padre Pio admonished her about this and warned her to be on her guard.

Rina, a musician friend of Mary's, used to come to San Giovanni Rotondo on such special occasions as feast days and Padre Pio's anniversaries. Rina liked the room given her in Mary's house and one day said to Mary; "Why don't you give this room to me? I could put my furniture and personal belongings in it, and it would always be there when I visit. It would be my room!" Rather than give Rina an answer right away, Mary told her she would decide before Rina left.

Several days later, it was time for Mary's confession to Padre Pio. By custom, after the sacrament had been given, a person was allowed to ask his or her confessor for advice; so, when Mary told him of Rina's request, Padre Pio said: "My daughter — now, Rina wants a room; next she will want an additional room. Then she will ask for the entire second floor. . . . Eventually, she will want the first floor, too, and finally the entire house. It will only end with you being put out of your house!"

Mary gave Rina her answer: Padre Pio advised her not to give up any of the rooms in her house, because they were needed for her use and for the members of her household, as well as other guests. Rina immediately grasped that if Padre Pio had advised Mary in this matter, that must be the final answer — and it was!

Mary always gave of herself to everyone, and everyone always gained the impression that they were personal friends of hers. At the hotel where my sister and I stayed, we often met people from various countries — France, Belgium, Ireland, and so on — and people would often say to us, "We have come to see Padre Pio and our dear friend, Mary Pyle."

Guiliana Monni, a local woman, told us that Mary's door was open to everyone. On numerous occasions Mary contributed her time, effort, and money to such charitable organizations as Youth Action Groups, to missions, to the Catholic University, to the seminary, and to the local parish. She never refused a worthy cause. As Guiliana remembered, Mary did not manage money; she made offerings through members of her household. Sometimes there was no money in the house; other times, she would send to Father Raffaele, the superior of the monastery at the time, for funds. On still other occasions, she called on her trusted household manager, Carmela. When Mary could not obtain money immediately, she would ask to be excused, requesting that her caller come another time, at which time Mary expected to be able to make a donation.

Gaetanina

ON a trip to San Giovanni Rotondo in 1958, my sister and I met Gaetanina, a woman aged about thirty-one, who was from central Italy. Of average height and build with brown curly hair and eyes and a round face, Gaetanina had a jovial, pleasing personality. She had run away from home because her mother had tried to force her into an arranged marriage. She had come to Padre Pio's monastery primarily because of her uncle, Fra Gerardo, a brother in the friary.

Gaetanina went to Padre Pio for advice, and he suggested that she apply to Mary Pyle for sanctuary and employment. When Mary heard that Padre Pio had sent Gaetanina, she immediately accepted her as a member of her household. Gaetanina was such a happy, young person, and liked to sing while she worked, that Mary called her "songbird" or "breath of spring."

Gaetanina assumed her responsibilities and share of the work of Mary Pyle's house. One warm, sunny day around noon, Helena and I arrived at Mary's to find Gaetanina washing linens on the patio. As we neared her, we smelled the sweet perfume we had come to associate with Padre Pio. The perfume was characteristic of the clothes and, sometimes, of the objects he touched.

"Gaetanina," my sister said, "you are washing Padre Pio's white alb, aren't you?"

"How do you know?" Gaetanina said, laughing. "By the smell of his perfume!" Helena and I answered in unison.

Gaetanina never told us why she had left home. Nor did she tell us that her mother and family no longer communicated with her. That year, when Helena and I returned to our teaching jobs in the United States, we also left Gaetanina, the new addition to Mary's household. In April of the next year, Mary wrote us:

Helena and Dorothy,

Here comes the sad note. Do you remember Gaetanina, Fra. Gerardo's pretty young niece who has been in my house for the last seven years? She was the youngest, prettiest member of our household. She seemed so healthy and full of life that I (called) her . . . "songbird"; other times (I called her) "breath of spring." Last May, she began to have trouble; and rapidly she got worse and had to admit she could not continue without a visit to a doctor. The visit and examination (showed) that she had cancer of the rectum. The doctors tried to operate, but there was nothing to be done. . . . She spent about a month in the hospital, but she wanted to come home to our house.

I wanted a second opinion of her case and had a renowned specialist, Dr. Nicolas DeSantis, come to see her. (He) confirmed the diagnosis, (adding that it was an advanced case and terminal, and he held out little hope, though he did suggest therapy in the meantime.)

Gaetanina died on March 18, a half hour before the feast of St. Joseph, after eight months of terrible suffering endured with real Christian resignation worthy of a spiritual daughter of a saint. It is pretty hard for a (woman of thirty-two), a normal girl who wanted to marry, etc., to suddenly realize that she (is) condemned to death, and with such suffering . . . she herself longed to be released. Padre Pio says that she is already in heaven. She will pray for us. . . .

Our beloved Padre Pio is very tired and has been suffering (from) earaches. I am afraid that you . . . are not praying enough for him. He told one of his spiritual children that it is true that he takes the responsibility (for) their souls but that they also have a responsibility towards him, because they must help with their prayers. Pray, pray, pray!

Padre Pio and Our Lady of Fatima

IN 1956, Mary told us, when the Pilgrim Virgin of Fatima came to Italy to begin a pilgrimage to various cities in Italy, Padre Pio, having offered himself as a victim for the conversion and salvation of souls, became very ill.

Diagnosed as having a fatal, cancerous tumor, he suffered much, and for several months was unable to celebrate Mass.

During this time, however, he was brought daily to a window, where, by means of a loudspeaker, he gave the day's exhortation.

Meanwhile, on August 6, the statue of Our Lady of Fatima arrived in San Giovanni Rotondo by helicopter and was placed on a high altar in Our Lady of Grace's church. The altar, banked with flowers and many candles, was surrounded by pilgrims from the towns and villages of the Gargano. Aware of Padre Pio's weakened condition, the father superior of the monastery suggested that the Pilgrim Virgin be taken to Padre Pio's room; but Padre Pio refused, saying he would go to her instead. Supported by two Capuchin friars, he walked to Our Lady and kissed her feet. Next, he placed in her hands a golden rosary he had received from his spiritual children in Florence (the rosary is now kept at Fatima). Then, with tears in his eyes, Padre Pio prayed in recollection.

Later, as the Virgin was borne away by helicopter, Padre Pio, held by two friars, stood at a window of the friary choir. As he watched the helicopter hover over the shrine and listened to the cheering pilgrims, Padre Pio burst into tears. With filial trust, he said: "Mother mine, you have come to Italy and brought me this sickness. You came to visit me and found me still suffering from it. Now, off you go, without even leaving me a blessing!"

As Padre Pio spoke this sorrowing complaint, a miracle occurred. Padre Pio later said that a shudder immediately ran through him. His body was penetrated by a flow of life. He felt the tumor burst and, from the waste caused by his long illness, flower again. "Let me go," he cried out. "I am healed! Our Lady has healed me!"

"Thank the Virgin of Fatima for me," Padre Pio subsequently wrote to a spiritual daughter. "On the very day that She left here, I felt well again. I have been back to celebrate Holy Mass since three days ago."

Another Letter to Carmelita

MARY Pyle's letters to those who corresponded with her usually revealed events centering on Padre Pio. They were a means of expressing her feelings about these events. The following letter was written to my sister, Carmelita, who at that time lived in Youngstown, Ohio, on the fiftieth anniversary of Padre Pio's ordination into the priesthood.

March 8, 1960

Dear Carmelita,

Thank you for your great generosity in giving for Padre Pio's jubilee. How beautiful your presents looked in the exposition of the gifts! . . . So many things are happening that we cannot understand and far less explain. Our beloved Padre Pio has offered himself as a victim to save the wicked world and takes all the faults of others upon himself and tries to seem the opposite from what he really is — to save others — to give up that which would be dearest to him — the affection and esteem of his brothers and superiors — Oh, how I am suffering to see that they do not understand him, but he always asks for suffering and, of course, that is the greatest suffering for him, and we take part in his suffering.

For your ears only, I tell you that we at this . . . moment are directly under the Pope and do pray with all our heart that he really understands our great and marvelous Father.

I hope that you received the little package with the jubilee souvenirs. (That) which I am enclosing is the one which he wrote, and he mentions his spiritual children. The crucifix in the back is the one in front of which he received the stigmata. Read, between the lines — we are suffering — we can never thank God enough to have given us such a Father — I send you his blessing and my love and lots of it.

Mary Pyle

The following is taken from a letter in which Mary Pyle gave an acount of the visit of Our Lady of Fatima statue and the cure of Padre Pio.

August 25, 1959

Dearest Carmelita,

How good God is to have given us back Padre Pio through the intercession of His Mother. . . . From April 24, 1959, Padre Pio was ill with double pleurisy (the liquid was removed eight times) until the statue of Our Lady of Fatima was brought by helicopter To San Giovanni Rotondo on August 5 . . . and She left on August 6, after have been exposed in the beautiful new church all night and having visited the sick in the hospital. She flew from the roof of the hospital in the helicopter and passed very low over the small monastery church where Padre Pio was kneeling and praying. As the helicopter flew away, Padre Pio said he felt a tremor and said Our Lady of Fatima (had) cured him. On August 10, he (was) praying at the altar of the new church and has been celebrating Mass ever since.

When are you coming back to see us?

Love,
Maria Pyle

Pope John XXIII's Pontificate

THE pontificate of Pope John XXIII, whose secular name was Angelo Roncalli, lasted from 1958 to 1963. It was one of the most intense and innovative pontificates of modern times. In the brief space of five years, events of great importance took place, such as the Ecumenical Council and the publication of the encyclicals *Pacem in Terris* (Peace on Earth) and *Mater et Magistra* (Mother and Teacher).

As Papal Apostolic Nuncio in France soon after World War II, then Angelo Cardinal Roncalli had several meetings with Emanuele Brunatto, a financier from Turin and an adherent of Padre Pio. John XXIII's attitude as Pope was not considered favorable to the friars of the Gargano, however; for it was widely believed that this attitude had resulted from the numerous complaints about the activities of those around Padre Pio that the Vatican received.

Pope John XXIII sent an emissary, Monsignor Carlo Maccari, to San Giovanni Rotondo. From the monsignor's recommendations issued the restoration of the "Franciscan rule" in the monastery. Through use of the rule, the Vatican sought to avoid the mass-hysterical scenes that often occurred during Padre Pio's Masses and to squelch what the Vatican considered the sacriligious commerce in bloody linen clothes. Monsignor Maccari spent three months at the hermitage of Padre Pio and was dismayed by what he learned. As punishment, the monsignor transferred to Cerignola Father Giustino of Lecce, one of those closest to the friar; and arranged for chains to be placed in front of Padre Pio's confessional and in front of the altar whenever Padre Pio celebrated Mass. The chains were to be removed only after Padre Pio had left the altar.

Later, Mary, in relating to Helena and me the story of

Monsignor Maccari's investigation, told us that when the monsignor made his report on the activities at the monastery that was related to Padre Pio, Pope John XXIII had replied: "They have chained the saint and . . . let the wild beasts out!"

The 50th Anniversary of Padre Pio's Ordination

ON the fiftieth anniversary of Padre Pio's ordination to the priesthood, Padre Pio received a letter from Giovanni Battista Cardinal Montini (later Pope Paul VI) filled with expressions of esteem and regard. "In Christ," Cardinal Montini said, "I wish to express my felicitations for the immense gifts (given) you, which you have dispensed to the faithful."

When in 1963 Cardinal Montini became Pope, Mary told us, one of the first things he did was throw out all cases against Padre Pio.

Father Karol Wojtyla

IN 1947, a young Polish priest named Karol Wojtyla came to visit Padre Pio. Father Karol was accompanied by two young priests. They were guests at the monastery, and after two days left. Just before leaving, however, one of the priests accompanying Father Karol visited Mary Pyle and, during their conversation, told her that Father Karol had told members of the community that he had confessed to Padre Pio, who afterwards predicted that someday the young Polish priest would be Pope and that during his papacy there would be violence and bloodshed! "If Padre Pio predicted this, it will happen," Mary Pyle said. "But who knows when it will be."

On October 16, 1978, Karol Cardinal Wojtyla became Pope John Paul II. And, indeed, as we all know, there was violence and bloodshed, as well as an attempt on Pope John Paul's life, Mary 13, 1981.

Illness

THE years pass, though, and even those totally immersed in good works in the service of the Lord — even those like Mary Pyle, who have throughout their lives been resistant to disease and harsh living conditions — begin to feel the effect of time and physical wear and tear. In November 1964, at age seventy-six, Mary was struck by unexpected illness. The illness would remain with her until the end of her life. Above all, she felt that Sister Death was near. Mary called the Capuchin director of her affairs and consigned to him her spiritual testament, together with a letter containing her last wishes. "Behold, O Lord," she exclaimed, "I am ready for life or for death."

Despite her infirmity, Mary continued to attend Mass and to take Holy Communion. For her, these were vital practices that must be performed each day. Both Mary's physician and the overseer of her household, Carmela Marocchino, suggested that, because of her illness, Mary should give up attending the 5:00 a.m. Masses of Padre Pio.

"I prefer to die rather than give up Holy Mass!" Mary replied heatedly.

Her illness so weakened Mary that her spiritual director told her: "From now on, you will go to Mass only on Sundays and holy days. On the other (occasions) you will receive Holy Communion in your house." Mary, bowing her head in obedience, said, "Fiat" (Thy will be done).

Even in sickness Mary was an inspiration to all. She was told — and she understood — the seriousness of her condition, that she could not continue in all her previous activities. What seemed to disturb her most was that others now had to be concerned about her even in the most mundane matters. Mary, wanting to avoid that, found a way to transform the situation into one of humiliation for herself. She remained in her house — in her room — in prayer and conversation with visitors.

On those Sundays when she felt well enough to go out, Mary took a cab to church. Her only regret was that she could not assist at daily Mass.

Throughout relapses and a worsening condition, she never complained, but continued to greet everyone with a smile and a cherring word. However, she continued her charity to the needy, which now, of necessity, was done through others.

In January 1965, Mary wrote a note to Carmelita, telling her about her illness.

San Giovanni Rotondo
1-12-65

Dearest Carmelita,

I thank you, also in Padre Pio's name, for everytthing and send you his blessings for all our friends and his spiritual children.
Did you know that I have had a slight stroke and am unable to move around? . . . . only with great difficulty do I occasionally succeed in going up to our beloved church. I love you more than ever, and send you Padre Pio's blessing.

Yours
Mary Pyle

Father Costantino told us that even then, Mary Pyle had been ill for a long time. When he visited San Giovanni Rotondo, he felt he should visit her. After a brief announcement, she asked to see him. He found her in her room, seated in an armchair next to the bed. Fearing that he would soon tire her, Father Costantino expected to remain only a few minutes. Mary, however, wanted to confide certain things to him.

She spoke, above all, of the suffering of her spiritual father, Padre Pio, of his trials, of the fact that for some time the religious province of the Capuchins had been the target of oppression and humiliation. As Mary spoke, her breathing became labored; her voice grew weak, and her face was marked by deep emotion. At various intervals, her eyes filled with tears.

Father Costantino listened silently, admiring and moved by a soul so good, fraternal, and uplifting.

In a voice broken by sobbing, Mary exclaimed: "And why am I so sick?" Mary, it turned out, was sick for the love of Padre Pio and the Capuchins. It was a sickness from which she would not recover. She had lived the heroic life of a true spiritual daughter. Father Costantino instinctively looked into her eyes, he said; and there he saw what seemed to be true radiance.

Mary's Health Declines

FOUR years passed before we returned for a visit. We found Mary older (in more ways than one). As her health deteriorated, her activity necessarily decreased. Others took over for her, and we still helped Mary compose a few letters each day, though we no longer spent hours answering them.

In June of that year, when my sister was again admitted to Padre Pio's hospital for treatment, I was left as Mary's only

"English" secretary. One morning after Padre Pio's Mass, Mary fainted in church. Medical attention was soon obtained, and she was sent home to rest.

A few days later, when I stopped by for a visit, I found her resting upstairs. We talked. After awhile she said she would like to answer "just a few letters," which we did. A short time later, I was called out of the room, leaving her in apparent good spirits. But when I returned a half-hour later, I found her in tears! "Mary, what happened?" With tears in her eyes, she replied: "Padre Pio appeared to me in bilocation, and I scolded him about letting me faint in church!" I pressed her for details, but she would not reply and changed the subject.

That year, a new, expensive organ was installed in the Church of Our Lady of Grace, and a professional organist was hired. Thus another activity was withdrawn: playing the organ in church. Other leaders had appeared and taken over direction of the Franciscan tertiaries. Meanwhile, the flow of visitors arriving to greet Mary increased. It seemed, however, that Mary felt the end nearing. Once, in my presence, she sent for two Capuchin fathers and spoke to them about making a final gift to her beloved project, the Capuchin friary at Pietrelcina, this one for a heating system and a new gymnasium for the seminarians.

The summer passed quickly, and soon it was time to say good-bye to our beloved Mary. Though we did not realize it at the time, this would be the last farewell.

In San Sebastian de Garabandal, Spain, a sixteen-year-old farm girl named Conchita Gonzales and two younger companions claimed to have had visions of Mary, the Mother of God, along with a message of prayer and penance similar to that received by the three children of Fatima. The event drew worldwide attention. Because of this claim, Conchita was invited to talk with Padre Pio. Following is Mary's account of the event.

February 7, 1966

Dear Carmelita,

Conchita, from Garabandal, came here with the daughter of the King of Spain. Padre Pio received them, but when he saw them, he said, "Oh, if I had known that you were dressed like that (in the short skirts in style at the time), I would not have come down." He is the only one fighting against (such) indecent styles. Again, much, much love,

Maria Pyle

When, because of advancing age, Padre Pio could not go to the community dining room with the other friars, he ate in his room with one of the friars for company (and to encourage and, if necessary, force Padre Pio to eat something). There was a time when Brother Lawrence, the cook, made gelatin for Padre Pio and noticed that he liked it. Naturally, there was always some left over, which the other friars ate. One afternoon about a year before Mary Pyle's death, Brother Lawrence asked: "Padre, may I take the gelatin left over to Mary Pyle?" and Padre Pio answered: "Yes, yes — if she deigns to eat it!"

Later that afternoon, Brother Lawrence hurried to Mary Pyle's house. He was shown to her room, but found that she was sleeping. His arrival with the food had alerted Mary, though, and, catching the new scent in the room, she wriggled her nose. "Who's there? Who's awakening me?"

"Maria, look," Brother Lawrence said; "this gelatin was passed over by Padre Pio. He sent it to you!"

Maria raised up and sat on the bed. Then, taking the gelatin, she ate it in one mouthful. Raising her arms heavenward, she said:

"Oh, Lord, how happy I am that Padre remembered me. Why has he done such an act of kindness as this?"

From then on, she instructed Brother Lawrence, when he prepared the gelatin for Padre Pio, to prepare some for her, and that the preparation of it be done in her house. This Brother Lawrence did for several months. Padre Pio had sent her a small gift, and now she wanted to reciprocate. It was as though it were an exchange of gifts!

In late 1967 and early 1968, Mary was consoled by visits from numerous relatives — her sister-in-law Dorothy, her niece Diana Pyle, an actress, two grand-nephews, a nephew and his wife, and her sister-in-law Zene. At Mary's suggestion, the relatives interested themselves in installing a heating system for the seminary gymnasium. (Two days before her death, Mary left the balance of her estate — thirty thousand dollars — for the heating system. The remainder of her earthly possessions were to go to the Capuchin fathers of Foggia, who had jurisdiction over the monastery at San Giovanni Rotondo.) Mary was content with the visit of her relatives. "This year," she said, "Padre Pio gave me such joy (in seeing) some of my relatives. Perhaps this will be the last year of my life. And then, what does it matter? I am old by now, (and) I must do the will of God!"

Earlier, when Mary became ill, she would say occasionally: "Without Padre Pio, I do not wish to stay, neither on earth nor in heaven." Once, though, she confided that Padre Pio had told her that she would die before him but that after a short interval he would follow her to the tomb. (In fact, he followed her barely five months after her death.)

Spring 1968

DURING the spring of 1968, Mary's last spring, her health became a series of anxious moments, so much so that Doctor Sale ordered

Mary Pyle: Under the Spiritual Guidance of Padre Pio 179

her sent to "La Clinica" (the popular name for La Casa Sollievo della Sofferenza, Padre Pio's hospital). "Send me to the clinic?" Mary replied. "No — I want to die on my own hard bed, in my house!" But, after seeking the advice of Padre Pio, who was of the same opinion as the doctor, she relented and permitted herself to be taken to La Clinica, where she was put under the care of Maria Salvatori, a nurse at the hospital and a friend of Mary. In agreeing to hospitalization, Mary had said she wanted Maria to be her private nurse. "Do not think, Maria, that I am afraid to die! I am ready, you know. If only the Lord would give me a little more time, if it pleases Him, as I have a few more things I would like to do. You know, Maria; I do not wish to remain (here on earth) without Padre Pio."

During the night of April 26, Mary said to Maria: "Do you think I will live until June? My relatives wrote to me, saying they will come to help me celebrate my eightieth birthday (April 17th)."

"Certainly," Maria answered. "Why not?" Mary had hardly finished uttering her question when she suddenly opened her eyes wide and stared into the distance. Then she closed her eyes again and tilted her head back. All was finished. Her life on earth was over. It was 11:00 p.m.

Maria rang a bell, and soon Mary's doctor and a nun arrived. The doctor examined Mary a moment, then said: "What did you call me to do? Mary Pyle is dead."

Mary lay with her eyes closed and her lips slightly parted. Maria the nurse, sent for the chaplain, Padre Innocenzo. Because it was now after eleven, however, he had retired for the night and had to be awakened. The Padre reached Mary's room some twenty minutes later, and quickly began the prayers of Extreme Unction, or last anointing. A moment later, Mary began to exhibit signs of life! Some of the color returned to her cheeks, but her eyes remained closed. Maria felt Mary's pulse and detected a beat. Then, almost under her breath, Mary said: "Even this is needed!"

It was as though her soul had returned to her body for the Extreme Unction. The sacrament was administered, and her body, at last, ceased to function.

Retrospective

MARY Pyle died at San Giovanni Rotondo at about 11:30 on the evening of Satuday, April 26, 1968, in the Home for the Relief of Suffering, where she had been taken on April 17, her birthday.

For some time, she had suffered from heart disease and had been obliged to progressively cut back on her activities. She was even deprived of the joy of visiting the church every day, and especially of attending Padre Pio's early morning Mass. Similarly, she had had to give up her work in the service of good. Her regret at having to do so could often be perceived, but her submission to the will of the Almighty would soon bring back a smile to her face.

Mary Pyle had been a faithful interpreter of the Franciscan ideal and of the example set by Padre Pio, whom she met in 1923 and had never again left.

Mary's home — the rose-colored dwelling set among almond trees, which in 1925 was the first house to break the monotonous barrenness of the area around the monastery — was like an adjunct to the monastery. In her home, she and her Franciscan tertiaries prepared the host for Communion; she studied hymns to be played at Mass and for other services, stamped and addressed envelopes for the monastery's considerable correspondence, and worked closely with the monks, many of whom she had known since they were youths, welcoming them into her house, encouraging them, and helping them in their studies. Numerous other monks from the province, not only monks but students of philosophy and theology, were accustomed to looking upon Mary as a surrogate mother. On visits to San Giovanni Rotondo, they went to see her and made a fuss over her, all in all, gladdening her life with wholesome Franciscan gaiety.

Mary's house was open to all comers at any time; all one had to do was knock at her door. When visitors did so, they frequently found her in the sitting room, at the end of a long table finished in dark varnish, with letters heaped in front of her. Gathered around Mary would be other guests and her tertiaries (whom she called her "household"), busy at ironing, sewing, or some other chore, while still others read. Rich and poor, illiterate and intellectual, from all parts of the world, sat side by side at her table, as Mary, serene and smiling, passed easily from Italian to English to French to German to Spanish. She always gave the impression of not noticing the large gatherings and the commotion around her.

At any moment, new visitors might arrive. Because of her great intelligence, she never knew the humiliation of degeneration, to the end keeping her vivacity, spirit, and serenity. Thus for forty-five years did Mary Pyle live in the shadow of Padre Pio.

We will always remember her like this — above the annulment of death — because that is how she was throughout her eighty years. That is how she lived, and that is how she died.

When I learned of Mary's death, I immediately thought of the day in 1962 when Helena informed Mary that she was donating a property in the United States to benefit the hospital. "You know," Mary replied, "I have been accused of not being (in favor of) the hospital. But it isn't true. I am *not* against it. What I object to is that some of the doctors (with the most difficult cases) go to Padre Pio and ask for his prayers. Some of them, before major surgery, ask Padre Pio to bless their hands. What happens is that, when, through Padre Pio's prayers, the surgeons are successful, they get the credit, and not Padre Pio!" Once, Mary said, she had mentioned this to Padre Pio, who said: "Mary, don't criticize the hospital, . . . it will be the place where you will spend your last days on earth!"

What Mary said about the hospital doctors was brought home

to my sister and me when we met a doctor in Foggia, who told us that he had worked in Padre Pio's hospital at one time but was so successful that he decided to leave and start his own practice. Then, when he was on his own, without recourse to Padre Pio's prayers, he became an ordinary doctor who saved some patients and lost others. The world did not beat a path to his door as he had thought it would!

Mary's Funeral

THE funeral was held at the Church of Saint Mary of the Graces. At Mary's request, seminarians came from all the Capuchin provinces of the area, as well as many friars. In attendance, too, of course, were people from San Giovanni Rotondo who had been helped by Mary Pyle at one time or another and whose lives were the better for her example.

The pallbearers consisted of six Capuchin fathers. Father Carmela di Donato, the father superior, gave the eulogy. He told his listeners that Mary Pyle's life, in its outward manifestation, had demonstrated clearly her union with God, that peace reigned in her heart. She would always be happy, always smiling, always calm. The poverty she had voluntarily accepted was clear for all to see, as was the gift of her riches that she had placed at the disposal of others. For forty-five years, Mary had lived austerely, in prayer and self-imposed poverty, attracted to the example set centuries earlier by Saint Francis. The Gargano Mountain to which she had been called, a place once rough and bare, was now a shining city. "There is not a single Capuchin monastery in our province," Father Carmela continued, "that has not received some gift from Mary. Above all, the monastery and church of Pietrelcina, where she worked and struggled, will stand as her monument. It was your desire, Mary Pyle, that your remains be placed in the Chapel of the Capuchins, with Padre Pio's family. This request we will fulfill.''

Throughout the service, Padre Pio, too weak to participate, nevertheless remained at the chapel. When given the news of Mary's cerebral hemorrhage and asked if he wished to visit her at the hospital, he had replied: "Physically, I am unable to do so; but I shall pray to the Lord that He take her to Paradise with the Angels.'' He reflected for a moment, then added: "She will finally be able to listen to the melody of the angels without having to play the organ!''

As the funeral cortege left the church, heading through the town to the cemetery, the monastery bells tolled. "I thank you, Mary Pyle, for the bread you always gave me," a woman of the village said in a loud voice. "I will pray always for you. Thanks! Thanks!''

Mary's body was laid to rest in the Chapel of the Capuchin Fathers, who had had inscribed on the tomb in gold letters:

OH MARY
FULL OF CHARITY AND OF SERAPHIC VIRTUES
REST FOREVER IN THE GRATEFUL MEMORY OF
PIETRELCINA TO WHICH YOU DONATED A MONASTERY
IN SAN GIOVANNI ROTONDO
WHICH FOR MORE THAN FOUR DECADES ADMIRED YOU
GENTLE SPIRITUAL DAUGHTER OF PADRE PIO
OF THE CAPUCHIN FATHERS WHO DESIRED TO HAVE YOU
IN THEIR CHAPEL

When Helena and I returned a few months later, we visited Mary's tomb and placed a floral wreath on it. In her home, we missed her presence and her warm hospitality. It was not the same without her.

Words from Padre Pio about Mary Pyle

CARMELA Marocchino, Mary's faithful servant for many years, told us of Mary's last days in Padre Pio's hospital, the Home for the Relief of Suffering. We asked her about the relationship between Padre Pio and Mary Pyle, and she said: "He said she 'was always a good religious (person), and the Lord knows who to give the just reward to those who have merited it.' "

Mary Pyle's earthly journey was over. She will be remembered by those who came to her for her kindness, gentleness, and charity and for her assistance in directing souls to Padre Pio. "The world will someday be surprised to know who Padre Pio really is!" she said once. May she continue her mission of directing souls to Padre Pio until the end of time!

Living continuously at the side of Padre Pio, whose advice she followed consistently, she performed splendid deeds of apostolicism, giving generously to the poor and those who suffered. Her house was the center for charitable deeds. The sorrows, persecutions, and triumphs of Padre Pio were hers as well.

Mary Pyle was a lighted flame. Generous benefactress and a true Franciscan soul, she was a pious, sincere Franciscan whose charity towards the poor, the sick, and the needy was renowned, earning her the gratitude of the Capuchin fathers and of all who knew her.

On September 6, 1971, in the monastery in Pietrelcina which largely through Mary's generosity and work had come into being, the Capuchin fathers of the religious province of Foggia dedicated a monument to "Mary Pyle, the American."

Memories of Mary Pyle

GERARDO Natale, a Capuchin brother, told us that for years he had suffered from asthma. For nights on end, he could not rest; nor could he stay in his bed, being forced to get up and walk through the corridors of the monastery.

One night, as Brother Gerardo was reflecting in his room on the great good that Mary Pyle had done for people during her life here on earth — especially for his niece, Gaetanina, who had been ill for more than eight months — a seemingly superhuman force suddenly caused him to have a beautiful inspiration: apply to Mary Pyle to help him, saying, "Mary, for the zeal that you had for the sick, when you were living, now that you are in Paradise, can you do something to stop these asthma attacks?" He then said three Hail Marys and retired for the night.

With the help of God, and through the intercession of his beloved Mary Pyle, Brother Gerardo's asthma attacks diminished in intensity and frequency, and he could again rest at night. Today, when he goes to the clinic in the morning, it is easy for him to walk; and he goes through his daily routine with tranquility.

He would always remember with gratitude, Brother Gerardo continued, having had his prayer heard through Mary's intercession. He related his experience over and over, so that others too might know about his unforgettable benefactress.

The house at the foot of the hill below the monastery permitted Mary Pyle to observe Padre Pio at close hand and to follow him. Being that close to the monastery meant that she could hear Mass every morning, that she could enjoy continuously Padre Pio's spiritual guidance, that she could help the Church and at the same time become a spiritual intermediary between Padre Pio and those who had come great distances seeking his help. Mary Pyle was, in fact, often the hostess. She presented visitors to Padre Pio. She consoled them when they were "haunted" by Padre Pio; persuaded them to return to Padre Pio; replied to their letters, in which, through her, they requested prayers and advice from Padre Pio. A polyglot, she spoke five languages fluently, acting as interpreter between Padre Pio and his foreign visitors. She conversed with visitors and later corresponded with them in their native languages.

Mary particularly liked to have people from the Church visit her in her house, especially priests, whom she treated in a spirit of faith as ministers of God. She wished the Capuchins well, and they, confreres of Padre Pio, responded by calling her their "mother." Mary had long since put her material possessions at the disposal of the Capuchins of Foggia, and the friars repaid her in the form of affection, esteem, recognition of her works, and the fulfillment of her final request: to be buried in the cemetery of their chapel in San Giovanni Rotondo.

Over the years, Padre Pio visited Mary's house many times. In addition, she had the honor of providing hospitality to Padre Pio's parents for a considerable period of time. It was in her house that they passed into eternity. Padre Pio's brother, Michael, and occasionally the cloistered nun Sister Pia were also guests in Mary's house.

Father Frederico Carozza, a Capuchin, considered Mary Pyle, under the spiritual guidance of Padre Pio, as a soul of exceptional moral stature. She had left the United States to come and live like a true daughter of Saint Francis — wearing the habit of the Franciscans, living in a small room, and sleeping on a hard bed. She had, Father Frederico said, a heart always open to the needy, and in her daily life constantly gave testimony of her lively faith, of her love for God, of her charity towards her neighbors. She was a daily communicant who loved prayer and penance. Poor in spirit, gentle, humble of heart, she conducted her life as testimony to the beatitudes. Mary was peace-loving, patient in the face of persecution, strong in every aspect of her life, and, in death, holy. Rather than lessening over time, the noble figure of Mary Pyle rose to great heights in a strange land.

In the Third Order of the Capuchin fathers of Foggia, the most notable figure was that of Mary Pyle, because she followed not only the voice of Saint Francis but that of Padre Pio as well, who, over more than forty years, transformed Mary Pyle's soul in seraphic ardor. From that memorable day when Mary met with Padre Pio, and after the first steps toward a continuing search for God, Padre Pio little by little saw in her countenance a recovery of serenity, an indication that she would accept his message and that of Christ, too.

Mary Pyle was a woman who hungered for sanctity and perfection, and for justice. In the Franciscan church of San Giovanni Rotondo, she found peace, serenity of spirit, and tranquility. Having happily bid good-bye to the world and all its pomp, to offers of marriage, she pronounced the religious vows of obedience, poverty, and chastity. In short, she became a living beacon of faith, a true source of charity.

In a continuous influx, an unforgettable spectacle, people came to her house in San Giovanni Rotondo from all parts of the world. There she comforted the poor and the sick, sinners and strangers, Italians, Americans. Brazilians, as well as those making their first steps toward conversion. Patiently and with great kindness, Mary led the last named to Padre Pio.

To all she gave the gifts of mercy as she calmed their hearts, relieved their suffering, illuminated the minds of those who had long been tormented. Although she too had experienced similar afflictions, Mary invariably exhibited understanding and compassion.

Father Gabriele Bove told us that he admired the faith and devotion of Mary Pyle not only toward Padre Pio but toward all priests. Almost instinctively, she would ask for a blessing or to kiss the hand of a priest (since Vatican II, the custom of kissing the anointed hand of a priest has become passe). On another occasion, Father Gabriele mentioned to Mary his regret at not having had the opportunity to have religious articles blessed by Padre Pio. "You bless them, Father," she answered decisively; "even in you is Jesus who blesses."

In conversation about priests, Mary was wont to say: "Who are we that we must judge the ministers of God?"

Another reminiscence of Father Gabriele's was of a gift Mary sent one Christmas to each member of the religious community. Like a mother sending gifts to her children, she said, "It is (imperative that I) think of the friars who have the care of my spiritual father, who sustain my soul in the walk (toward) perfection." It was the first time Father Gabriele had heard it from a Third Order Franciscan (the branch to which Mary Pyle belonged).

How can one forget the joyous spirit Mary Pyle, with her exquisite charity, gave to so many souls? If she had not, through her renunciation, followed the divine vocation, she would not have left the example she did, that of sublime virtue. Nor would she have realized the work that became associated with her name: building the monastery in Pietrelcina, donating money to the church that is a basilica, gathering the religious vocations, lending vitality to her house in San Giovanni Rotondo, which, with loving care she kept open to all.

To a large extent, the spiritual greatness of Mary Pyle depended on Padre Pio. It was from him that she learned truly to love God, to live as a Franciscan, to use her excellent qualities, culture, and material possessions to the best advantage. Mary Pyle was a triumphant example of Padre Pio's spiritual direction. He found in her great feeling and a precise reflection of his own interior life as a mystic and an authentic son of Saint Francis. Mary, as his spiritual sister, was for Padre Pio what Saint Clare had been for Saint Francis. She gave whatever she could to Padre Pio in the order of the spirit. From him she received a powerful impetus toward the most high God. Padre Pio, in turn, taught Mary the love of God and the love of neighbor. The faithful exercise of these precepts made of Mary Pyle a creature worthy of the glory of God and the veneration of all people.